Fractals and Faith

Patterns for Learning in Discipleship

James Klaas

DevEd International Inc

Cover art: "A conversation". Photo: Gord Jones

ISBN: 978-0-9878369-1-5

Dedication

To our six kids: Stand on our shoulders and live the Promise. We love you all.

"The smallest one will become a clan and the least one a mighty nation"

Isaiah 60:22

"I have no greater joy than this, to hear of my children walking in the truth "

3 John 3

Table of Contents

The Book at a Glance:

Section 1: Fractal, or reproducing patterns, define outcomes, are social and are essential for scale-up.

Discipleship is the process of learning from Jesus Christ. Design patterns are called fractals. We can combine these ideas to identify predictable patterns that form bigger structures that either contribute or work against discipleship. Personal and corporate patterns of discipleship in the church today need to be seriously considered.

Social learning fractals are reproducing social patterns that resemble fractals. In the church these affect how we learn expected behaviour such as dress code, seating arrangements, the amount and nature of our involvement and our response to sermons. The fractal Jesus used was a combination of public ministry and individual time with his disciples.

Scale-up is the process of moving from a small project to a large one. The church, in dealing with scale-up, replaces personal care in discipleship with corporate teaching. One unfortunate part of this pattern is that people may not realize what they are missing, thinking that the pattern of passively receiving information is normal expected behaviour.

Section 2: A Discipleship fractal contains the Jesus kernel and a discipleship cycle.

Part of the discipleship fractal, that is not open to change, we call the *unchangeable kernel*. We may think that everything we do as a church should fit here. Each need to decide what part of the Gospel is an unchangeable discipleship pattern and what part adapts to culture.

Jesus gave us a pattern we can imitate when he entered the world of those he wanted to reach in a process that can be summarized as "being with him". He chose twelve disciples for that purpose. Even his opponents recognized his disciples as having "been with him".

Section 3: Divine resources empower the fractal and involve promise claiming, the Scriptures and prayer.

The means to scale-up depends on God's resources so there is no 'energy shortage' when it comes to making disciples. The promises in the Scriptures start with longing, just like a baby, for the milk of the Word. They point us to receiving a spiritual inheritance that encompasses the nations. The practice of having a devotional time with another is an experiential learning technique that can help others grow. We can offer simple patterns for prayer to encourage new believers in their journey.

Section 4: The learning journey releases the discovery process and spins outward toward the world.

Some people must be coaxed, bribed and pampered to get them to learn something while others eagerly learn before they are even asked. Self-discovery in learning and taking ownership of the process challenges traditional internal messages about identity and learning. When this empowered learner connects with another of like-heart, a true friendship develops. This enables greater risk-taking in moving from theory to practice through experiential learning. Both are quick to learn, adjust and involve others.

Section 5: The Discipleship fractal must contain a compelling story, awakens passion and other key elements.

The story is like a sticky burr that causes the message to be remembered. It is extremely efficient by using few words to carry the meaning. We need a story that explains the discipleship fractal. In addition in order to respond with *compassion* (*feel with*) to a suffering world, we first require *passion*. Our communication must resonate with this passion, like the wine glass vibrating when the finger is traced around the lip. The discipleship fractal, containing the Kernel of the Gospel, must be driven according to divine resources and not in our own strength. It must involve a learning journey where learners own, share and surrender their journey together with others. Formal teaching must enable informal learning using methods adapted to learners' needs and preferences. It must be able to scale to accomplish the Great Commission. It is a daunting task but one which we observe in the methods and life of Jesus. He is our model, method and message.

Introduction

A disciple is a learner.

Our learning about Jesus and our relationship with the church follow certain patterns. Some of these are centuries old and some are newer. Some are clearly seen and some are below the surface exercising their influence in spite of what we do. Some are helpful patterns and some are not. In this book we will refer to these repeating patterns as, 'fractals'. Think of them as the DNA that is affects the design of what we do in our faith communities.

A disciple is a learner. To be a disciple of someone means you are dedicated to learn all you can from that person. It is like following that person as your guru and in fact that was the pattern that the disciples in Jesus' time used to follow him. Some might think it presumptuous to call oneself a disciple of Jesus rather than a Christian although disciple is by far the most common term in the New Testament to refer to His followers[1].

The purpose of this book:

The purpose of this book is to encourage you to:

- Recognize repeating fractal patterns in social learning structures.
- Determine the essential components of a discipleship social learning pattern.
- Develop tools that contribute to the development of these learning patterns.
- Construct a plan how these patterns can be used to multiply disciples on a larger scale.

Who is the book for?

Is this book for church leaders or members of a faith community? Both! Some of the fractals will involve a redesigning of roles between laity and clergy because everyone should have a voice in the decision-making process. How that happens depends on church structure. Certainly I hope that pastors and boards will discuss this. But we are all permitted to vote at annual meetings and we vote with our feet every time we attend or not. We have unspoken expectations that influence programming and we have various degrees of frustration as to 'why can't the system change?' Hopefully this book will call us to reflection.

It also should call us to dialogue as this book is not designed to just be read on its own. Discussion and reflection questions are included at the end of each chapter as well as there is a place to carry on the

[1] The term *Christian* is used only 3 times in the New Testament whereas the term *disciple* is used 282 times.

dialogue on the web[2] . There is a discussion forum for each chapter with additional resources. Please share questions, ideas, examples, tools and resources as well as resolve and motivation to learn.

This book should also call us to action, to dare to experiment as learners with new methods, following hunches, and listening as well as acting upon intuition and insights from Scripture. Whatever change is needed in the church is something we can only realize by 'learning our way through it'.

If we can do all of this in the space of this book, the objectives will be accomplished. Whether it will happen will depend on all of us. This process is really meant to spark a conversation. The ideas that surface from discussion will be far richer than anything presented here. We are learners together and I am trusting God to show us what we don't know, guide us in what we do understand and strengthen us in the formation of better patterns for being learners of Jesus ourselves and for helping others as they join us.

My greatest fear is that you conclude: "This is another impossible discipleship programme. I want something I can do; not something that points out once again where I fall short!" Would it help if I confessed, "This is not a programme. It is what I understand and believe right now. It will change next week after you help me learn." If nothing else, use my errors to find the best way forward. While I take full responsibility for all shortcomings both in the concepts and writing, I believe that even these can serve to help us gain clarity.

My greatest dream is that you would find this liberating, that you begin to recognize fractal patterns and choose the best ones, that you better understand how your story fits into The Story, and that you are given wings as a learner of our Lord Jesus. To God be the glory if that happens in some way.

I would like to thank family and friends who lovingly considered these thoughts with me. Your lives have been oxygen to my soul and I am always learning from you. This book is my offering back to you.

James Klaas

Guelph, ON, Canada

---

[2]ONLINE Instructions: First time users will have to register. We do this in order to reduce spam. Go to www.networkchurch.ca and scroll to the community discussion link. Open and go to "*Is this your first time here?*" and follow the instructions to open a new account. You will need to enter a *username* (what you will be called in the forum) and a *password* of at least four characters. You will need to confirm an email sent to your account. If it does not show up, check the SPAM folder for the confirmation email. Bookmark the access link for returning to the site. Once you are in the website, select *Fractals and Faith Book Discussion*.

Section 1: Fractals are Reproducing Patterns

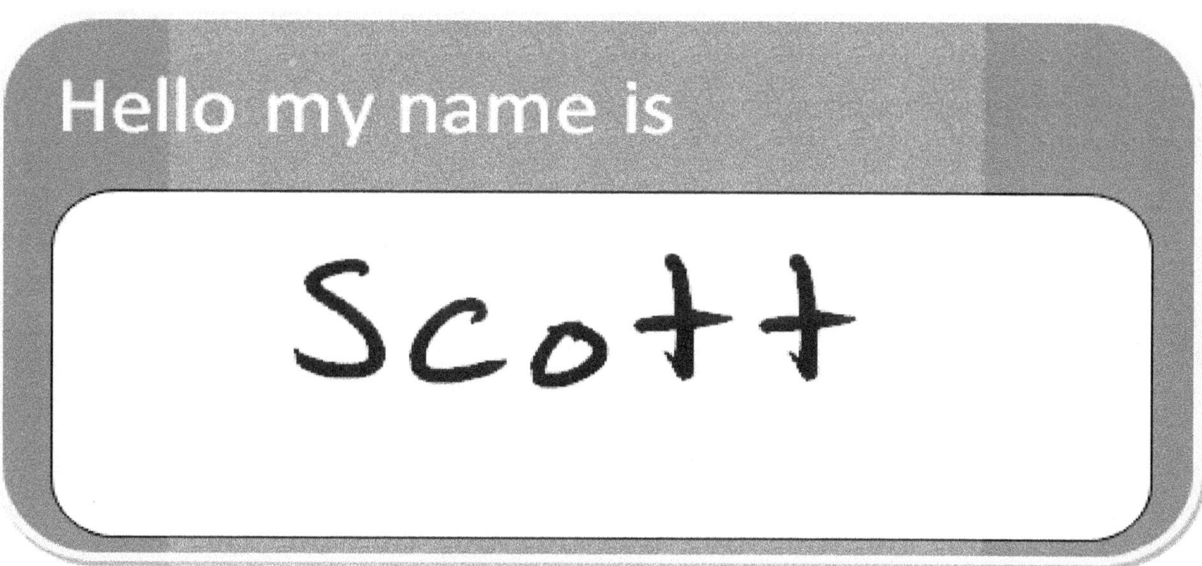

The "Hello my name is Blog" is probably the most helpful blog I read regularly. Over 10 years ago Scott Ginsberg decided to wear a "Hello my name is____" tag every day and everywhere he went. He even had a name tag tattooed on his chest. He built his whole zany brand around truly becoming the best you can be and refusing conformity to anything less. The name tag fractal captures perfectly the irony of what happens if we follow the crowd as our highest aspiration.

He makes an excellent point about learning to read patterns:

> Intelligence comes from pattern recognition, not information memorization....Remember: Life is easier, simpler – and ten times more profitable – when you get good at identifying patterns. What profitable patterns are just waiting to be discovered? (Ginsberg, Hello My Name is Blog, 2010)

In this section we will learn to recognize repeating patterns before looking at how it affects discipleship:

- Chapter 1 Fractals Determine Outcomes
- Chapter 2 Social Learning Fractals
- Chapter 3 Fractals and the Problem of Scale-up

Chapter 1: Fractals Determine Outcomes

Figure 1: Jim demonstrating the technique of how NOT to enter rapids.

Don't grab the gunwales!

I would love to be able to impress you with my white-water canoeing skills but one look at this picture tells the truth. I am breaking the cardinal rule by grabbing the gunwales when I should be paddling. We tipped shortly afterward much to the puzzlement of my companion in the bow. Naomi and I were taking a white-water course. The whole experience was nerve-raking and created some tension between Naomi and me. The instructor even developed special hand signals to help us calm down. The photographer suggested that I quietly lose this photo (figure 1). It is too good an example of "learning through failure" for me to throw it out.

There were clear patterns in the water to explain what happened and why we tipped. In canoeing lingo, there are stacks and troughs, which result from the volume of water influenced by the slope of the river, and the shape of rocks under the surface. These dynamics require the precise response of the paddlers (like holding on to the paddle and not the gunwales). We didn´t tip because we had bad luck or the river was being mean. We tipped because of the improper action of one of the paddlers in the canoe as it interacted with a pattern of the water. Experienced canoeists "read" the river patterns and know how to position their bodies in the canoe and what to do with the paddle. It will be true of a small stream or a mighty river; the same results can be predicted in the Arctic or the Amazon.

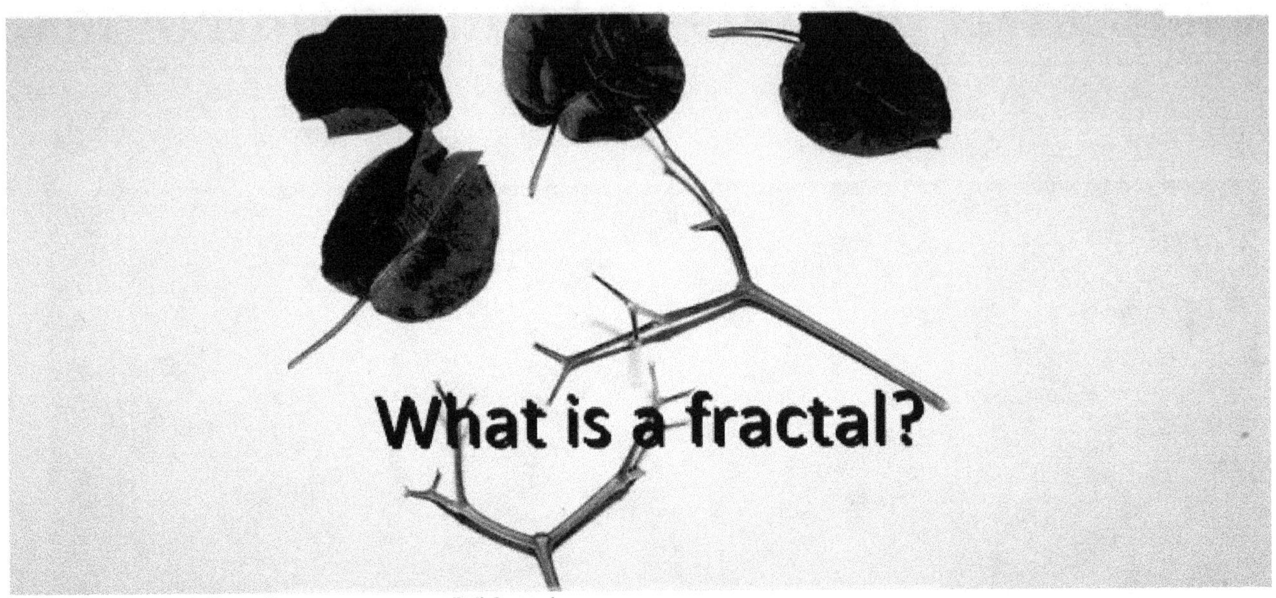

Figure 2: Bougainvillaea flower stems use a "Y" fractal

We can call these patterns 'fractals, a term coined by Benoît Mandelbrot in 1975[3], to denote a design component or shape that when repeated produces a larger structure which has "the same degree of irregularity on all scales. A fractal object looks the same when examined from far away or nearby..." (Mandelbrot, 1982).

These patterns are found in nature like the flower stems as shown in figure 2. It is also found in broccoli ferns, snowflakes and lightning. We can create fractals by a mathematical function that repeats itself as part of the process of creation. A "recursion" happens each time the cycle is repeated.

In the case of this flower stem (figure 3), the plant produces a 'Y' shaped branch in each cycle. Each arm of the Y produces another Y and so on.When a broccoli plant produces the first floret it will look exactly the same on a small scale as the finished head. The plant uses the fractal pattern to keep building more florets until the head is formed. It is 'easier' for the plant because it has a simple design that repeats over and over.

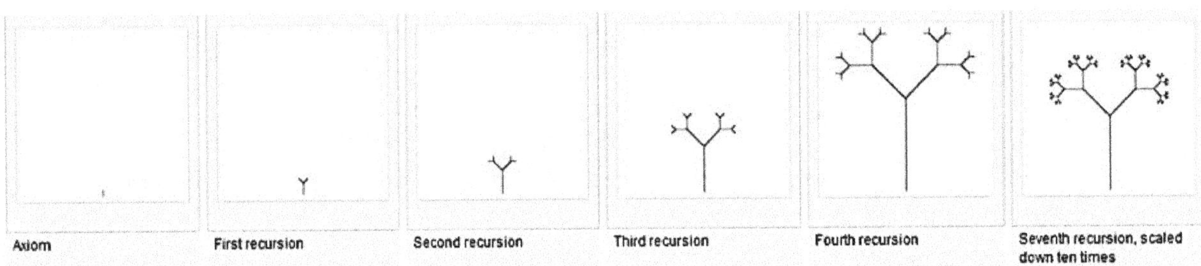

Figure 3: A series of recursions of the 'Y' fractal (source unknown)

An interview of Mandelbrot: http://www.ted.com/talks/benoit_mandelbrot_fractals_the_art_of_roughness.htm [3] and a 1 Minute Learner: http://www.devedinternational.net/1ml/1ml-085/player.html

Fractals in art and software

The art piece on the front cover of the book was designed as a fractal. I was impressed with some lily pads in a lake (figure. 4). It looked as though they were having a conversation. I wanted to use a fractal process to capture this as a piece of art. The fractal rule I used was an 'open circle shape' at each level of the design. I prepared the background first by using a slice of an old branch (on open circle figure 5) and pressed it into wet plaster. After it was painted, I applied and painted tissue paper cutouts of lily pad leaves. I also arranged the leaves in an open circle shape. The fractal became a story that helped me decide what to do next. The open circle symbolized the conversation among these leaves and the fractal provided depth and interest, creating a floating quality for the leaves over a dynamic liquid surface.

Figure 4: Lily pads that inspired art work

Figure 5: Wood used to texture plaster

Ferns are examples of fractal designs found in nature and we can use software to mimic their pattern. By varying the number of times the pattern is repeated (recursion) and the angles and lengths of branches, the controls at the base of figure 6, the plant design develops in markedly different shapes.

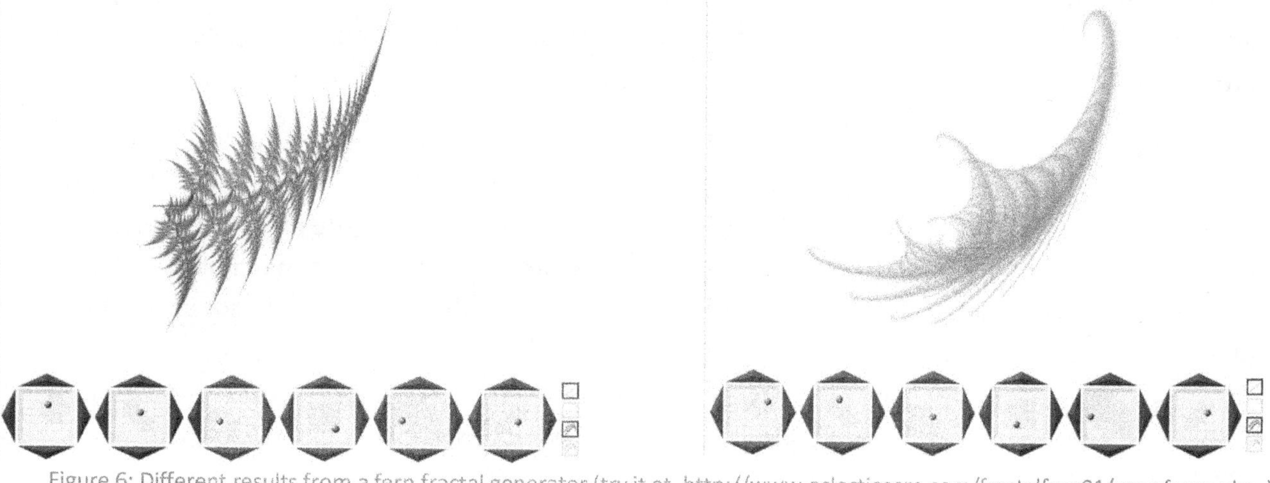

Figure 6: Different results from a fern fractal generator (try it at http://www.eclecticosm.com/fractalfern01/growferns.php)

Characteristics of fractals

Fractals have predictable characteristics. We can observe three characteristics of fractals that will help us in our consideration of discipleship. They are universal, consistent and extremely efficient.

Figure 7: Fractals found in nature.

Fractals are *universal*. We recognize patterns in nature around us. We are especially interested in those fractal-like patterns in human behaviour. Consider how a toddler learns to eat, a child learns to swing or ride a bike. We can examine these social learning fractals in more detail in the next chapter.

Fractals are also *consistent*. I have seen drifting sand in Sudan and drifting snow in northern Canada and the dunes/drifts look the same. The laws that govern their movement affect them both in a similar way and it doesn't really matter whether it is 40 below or 40 above zero , or whether it is sand or snow. It will be consistent whether the dune is small or large or if it is a little drifting snow or a blizzard. Size doesn't matter. Later on we will see the importance of this as it relates to going from a small-scale pilot project to something widely used. We will refer to this process as "scaling up".

We may only notice the fractal when the pattern gets broken. Soldier uniforms are not strict fractals, but the consistency of the pattern in the military is extremely important. When I was in the militia I got severe blood poisoning in my foot and the physician prescribed that I wear sandals for a few days instead of marching boots. I remember some hippies laughing at me as I waited for the bus. They called out, "Look at the soldier wearing Jesus boots!"[4] The inconsistency of the pattern attracted their attention.

Fractals are *extremely efficient*. If we can understand the design rules that control the change and how they repeat (See the controls at bottom of figure 6 in the fern example), then we can adjust the initial design to produce the desired outcomes. With each repetition of the design the pattern begins to emerge. Choose the correct pattern and the end result will be carried out with a minimum of effort. Choose the incorrect design elements and in spite of all the effort, the end result will not be as we intended.

[4] I am not using the Lord's name disrespectfully, as this was the protest term used by the hippie generation identifying Jesus as a non-conformist.

Fractals as an analytical tool for discipleship

I believe we are unaware of which fractals are operating in our churches. If we can recognize biblical patterns for making disciples, then we can reproduce these good patterns in our practices to replace the unhelpful ones. This assumes we are clear on what we are looking for.

Jesus never suggested 'adding in a little discipleship" to an overly crowded life as an option to improve satisfaction of the participants. He was not suggesting signing up for a course, attending a meeting or getting a post graduate degree. Rather he issued an all-encompassing call to leave everything (Matthew 10:37-39; Luke 9:23-25) and learn from him (Matthew 11: 28-30). Jesus presented discipleship as an all-or-nothing relationship that produced not only personal transformation but a history-changing world-wide movement. He required uncompromising prioritization of that relationship and accepted no rivalry.

We need to seriously consider what it means to keep at the job we have been given and not do something else. We may be tempted to add discipleship to the thousand activities of the church which is a sure recipe for trivialization of discipleship and burn-out of the leaders.

Just as Jesus assigned us this task, he kept another job for himself. He said he would 'build his church' (Matthew 16:18). One of the present day patterns that may be observed is our preoccupation with trying to do His job of building the church and neglecting our own job of making disciples. We have been much more consumed with church growth than making learners who follow Jesus.

We have tended to water down the interpretation of our responsibilities. Jesus commissioned us by saying "go and make disciples of all nations, baptizing them in the name of the Father and of the Son and of the Holy Spirit, and teaching them to obey everything I have commanded you. And surely I am with you always, to the very end of the age."

Note he said we should teach others to obey all that He commanded (emphasis added). We have conveniently reinterpreted this to simply *teach what He commanded*.[5] By omitting the 'obeying' component, we can teach lots of information and avoid the difficult part of obedience.

We assume that transfer of information will somehow result in changed behaviour. But we are caught in such an information deluge that it is becoming increasingly more difficult to keep it all sorted out. We simply hope that "a miracle occurs" (which sometimes happens) without reflecting on whether this learning pattern is the best. Teaching patterns need to be designed for behaviour change.[6]

We need to discover the fractals that promote disciple-making and which ones to avoid. Fractals are clearly evident in the church, in society and in the Scriptures (chapter 2). We will look at the particular problem of 'scaling up' our methods and which fractals work at cross-purposes to discipleship (Chapter 3). The structures we create are perfectly designed to give the results we have. If we want different results, what are we going to do differently?

---

[5] I am grateful to Al Middleton of Dynamic Churches International for this observation.

[6] See (Jefferson, V.H.Pollock, & Wick, 2009) for business sector example on training to change performance.

In Section 2, we will look at the discipleship fractal which includes the unchangeable Jesus kernel (chapter 4) and the discipleship cycle (chapter 5).

Section 3 discusses the Scriptural resources that empower our discipleship: claiming the promises of God (chapter 6), as well as listening to God in the Scriptures and in prayer (chapters 7 and 8).

Section 4 explores the learning journey that accompanies our discipleship: Learner Agency (chapter 9), collaborative connection in micro-teams (chapter 10) and risk agility (chapter 11) as the three main dynamics that release us to learn.

Section 5 examines the role of story (chapter 12), communication (chapter 13) and suggests a possibility for assembling the discipleship fractal (chapter 14).

I will not present a discipleship programme, nor give the final word on the best materials to use. I am hoping these suggestions, questions and activities will stimulate personal observations and discussion relevant to each local context. My commitment is to learn as best I can with the Bible as our guide and believing that God will lead us to a deeper understanding and ability to make disciples of all nations.

For discussion:

1. Watch the experiential learning video from YouTube[7] (Klaas J. H., 2007). How is "canoeing in rapids" similar to the discipleship process?
2. Can you think of examples of fractals not mentioned in the chapter? (Try doing a web search and see what you can discover.)
3. What fractals are involved in discipleship as you understand the term? List verses and observations as well as questions you hope to address.
4. Do you observe any reproducing patterns that work against discipleship?

For personal reflection:

What is the fractal pattern of your discipleship as you follow Jesus?

[7] http://www.youtube.com/watch?v=mToQGltYXd8

Chapter 2: Social Learning Fractals

Figure 8: The author riding his bike around the church auditorium during a sermon.

If we took a survey on how you learned to ride a bike, how many of you learned in a formal course taught at school? I suspect none of you. An older sibling may have helped, or your parents might have given you a small bike with training wheels after you graduated from a tricycle. At some point they took the training wheels off, ran behind the bike holding the seat, yelling encouragement, THEN LET GO. You probably wobbled a bit, crashed once or twice, scrapped a knee or two and then triumphantly were riding on your own. And you very likely went on to teach other friends, nieces and nephews or your own children the same way. No one organized it, there was no programme; it just happened because you probably pestered your parents for a bike and one spring day you learned to ride.

I call this a' social learning fractal'[8]; a pattern where through informal social interaction learning is transferred from person to person and generation to generation. It is self-organizing[9] and without complicated rules. It may be supplemented by a formal seminar at a school or park on traffic rules or

---

[8] You could argue this is an inexact use of the term *fractal* since a bicycle rider is not made up of many little bicycle riders, or the group of bicycle riders is not in the shape of a single rider, but it is used here to reinforce the idea that the pattern of learning is repeated as an informal self-reproducing pattern.

[9] See the 1 Minute Learner on self-organizing learning: http://www.devedinternational.net/1ml/1ml-078/player.html and http://www.devedinternational.net/1ml/1ml-079/player.html

bicycle safety and proper tools like appropriate bike size, helmet and training wheels. However, learning happens through a social and experience-based process which is easily passed on. The social component is essential in the learning process.

Another example of a social learning fractal is teaching children to eat with a knife and fork. Consider the steps leading up to that:

- Exclusively breastfed for the first six months.
- Children are fed by another person where they only have to open their mouths, chew and swallow. At first the food is completely soft. New foods are introduced little by little, based in part by the child's interaction with the adult, and the baby's tolerance and preferences.
- Children are given food on their tray: cheerio's, small pieces of soft fruit, cut-up pieces of vegetable and meat which they eat with their fingers.
- Children are given more complicated foods and a small spoon with a big handle and bowl with high edges.
- More complicated utensils are introduced and eventually the child can handle a knife and fork where more complicated etiquette rules are explained and encouraged.

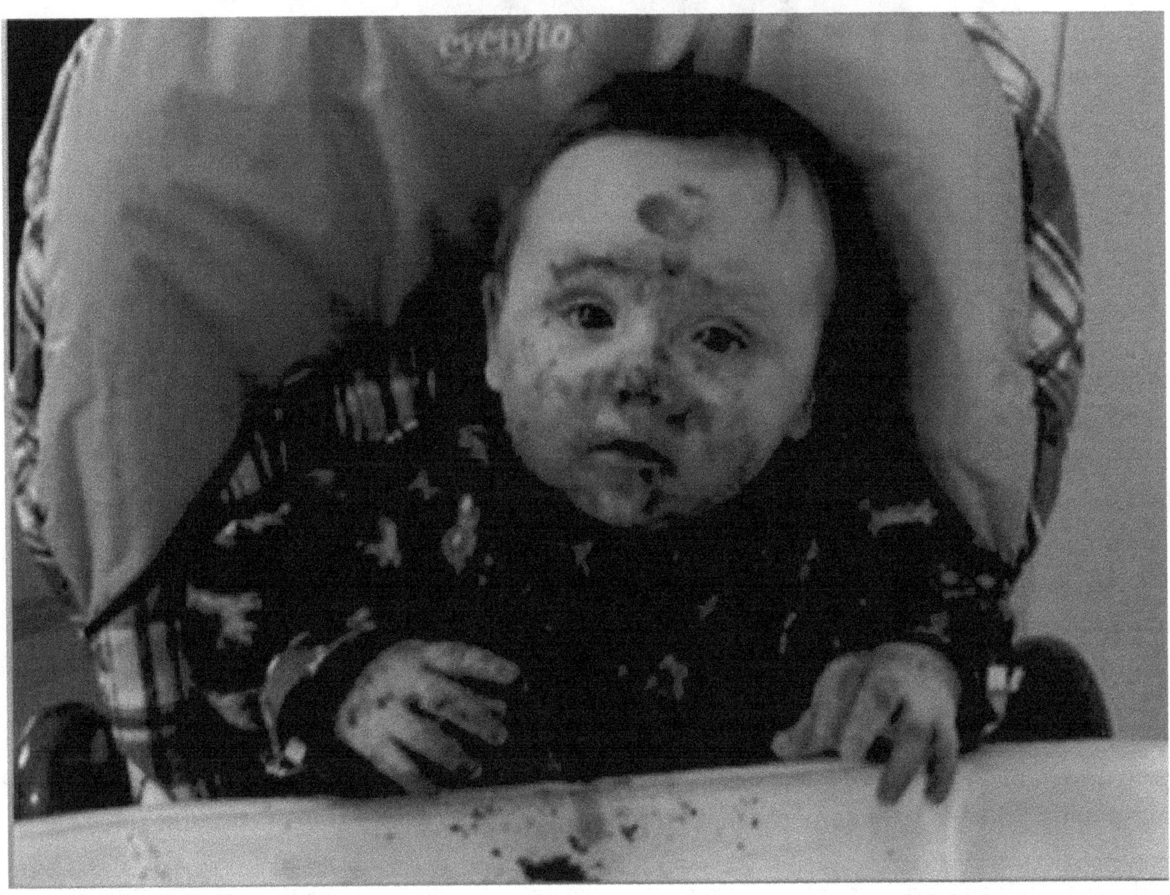

Figure 9: Learning to eat is a messy process. Photo: Chris Milne.

The process is highly experiential, messy and extremely social. It is repeated at least three times a day for years. Everyone learns from the process: just look under the highchair where the pets gather for scraps! Watch how adults open their mouths to prompt the child with supportive words and happy sounds. A formal course is never used rather a social learning pattern is repeated and passed on.

Figure 10: Active feeding improves child's health. Photo: Barbara Main

There are also some troubling social learning fractals in our culture. Virtual realities where young men invest 10,000 hours playing violent video games are restricting their ability to relate in the real world. They disengage with dictated school activities because they are bored. This results in social isolation outside of their virtual reality (Zimbardo). Contrast this with the 10,000 hours it takes to become an expert in a valued skill [10] and one can imagine how these boys will struggle to find a productive place in the system.

Positive family interaction is disappearing where only twenty percent of Americans regularly sit down for meals together. The key finding of a 2010 study conducted by the National Marriage Project at the University of Virginia indicates that divorce, non-marital childbearing and unmarried cohabitation have led to a dramatic increase in "fragile" and "typically fatherless" families over the past five decades[11]. These patterns are quietly reproducing themselves and becoming the norm for typical family interaction. We could label them damaging social learning fractals.

Social learning fractals in the church

There are many examples of social learning fractals that apply to organizations: expected behaviour, dress code, time and day of meeting and seating patterns. These are rarely taught formally but are learned by imitation and passed on generation to generation. They often make up the environment that cause people to recognize something as 'church'. Seating patterns where people all face forward may be very efficient for use of space but people can sit near each other for years and never learn the other's name. We can depend on the announcements of events to encourage participation in programmes instead of personally reaching out to another to encourage their involvement. Sometimes we deliberately try to change the pattern by asking people to stand and greet each other or make a photo

[10] (Gladwell, 2008, p. 288)
[11] (Wilcox & Marquardt, 2010)

directory with names. The problem is that unless a person gets involved in the activities outside of Sunday morning, they can remain 'unknown' in spite of the programme.

Sermons are a teaching pattern that are not really a social learning fractal since the majority of people who listen to them, do not in turn give sermons (the pattern is not repeated). We would better label it as a formal pattern where one person does the talking and the rest listen, often with no interaction. But *our reaction to the sermon* has a recognizable fractal component that is passed on to others. How we are expected to respond is repeatedly taught informally and is repeated.

I can name sermons that I have heard years ago that were formational in understanding salvation and service, even in going overseas as a missionary. When I first came to the church and heard the Bible clearly taught I thought it was fantastic. I wanted to learn everything and attended every service I could to learn more. Consider the sharp sword that comes from Jesus' mouth.[12] This sword cuts to 'joints and marrow ...and discerns the thoughts and intentions of the heart'.[13] I experienced that as a young believer and do so to this day. In our exposure to the Scriptures, we are to become effectual doers and not hearers only.[14] The Bible is meant to be taken very seriously.

After my initial orientation to the Bible I recognized a problem. I noticed it was progressively more difficult to remember what was taught and to try to apply it before I received a new teaching. Often I couldn't remember what was taught even on the way home from church. After a while, I wondered if anyone really expected me to remember and apply the sermon. I found if I just showed up, sat down and did not say anything, everyone was happy. It was a lot easier to sit quietly rather that struggle to remember, ask questions, disagree about something or search the Scriptures on my own. I quickly picked up the social learning fractal of a passive response to the sermon. Listening to it was an end in itself.

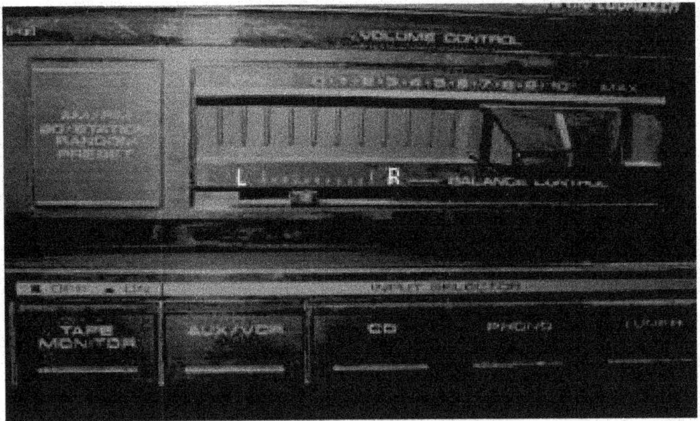

Figure 11: Slider bar for left and right stereo speaker

I am not sermon bashing. Jesus gave sermons: on the mount, on the plain, from a boat and as circumstances allowed. But what else did Jesus do for learning? How much time did he spend with his disciples walking, sleeping, eating, talking, asking questions, serving and reflecting together? How much time did he discuss the parables with them after he spoke to the crowds without explanation? What did he tell them about the Pharisees' anger and opposition? How many questions did he ask? The disciples observed him, requested help, complained or tried to give Him advice. It was very interactive.

---

[12] Revelation 1:16
[13] Hebrews 4:12
[14] James 1:22-27

This balance between disciple and crowd interaction can be illustrated with the analogue slider found on old stereos (figure 11) used to select how much volume goes to the left or right speaker. Depending on where you slide the button, more sound would go out one side or the other. Jesus seemed to have a stereo strategy for teaching the crowds and the disciples. Did Jesus spend half his time with the crowds and half with the disciples?

I recently asked a congregation of about 500 to vote on how they felt Jesus divided his time between teaching the crowd and teaching his disciples. I had made it clear that I didn´t know the answer so people should feel free to vote exactly as they thought. The majority by far felt he spent at least eighty per cent of his time with his disciples and twenty percent with the crowds.

Where would you move the slider? I don't think we can say exactly but I am pretty sure the slider would be much nearer the time spent with the disciples than with the crowds. For every hour delivering a sermon, Jesus probably spent dozens of hours with the twelve.

How does our particular church structure promote discipleship compared with what Jesus did with the disciples? Today we might find His example totally impractical or impossible. We can't take three years to be day and night with the twelve and so we rely on sermons to make up the difference. All the sound is coming out of one side of the stereo while the other is silent. We have pushed the dial too far to one side.

I asked the same congregation to vote on how they divided their own time between their public ministry and ministry to their disciples. I was shocked that almost no one was willing to vote and I asked them why.

One person said, 'This question requires a lot of thinking. I am not sure how what we do, fit into making disciples or if it relates to the ministry to the crowds. We have it all mixed together.' It was a very good point as this is a different way of thinking about church structures, programmes and where we put our emphasis.

The challenge is to find the self-reproducing patterns that empower people, help them apply the learning and enable them to pass it on to others in the disciple- making process. We will offer suggestions on how to do this later in the book.

For discussion:

1. It is often said that people happily listen to sermons in order 'to be fed'. In what ways is this a good pattern and in what ways could this be a problem?
2. What was the sermon topic last week? One month ago? How did you apply it? What were the expectations to apply it? What does Scriptures say about being only hearers of the Word?
3. If we wanted to make an optimal social learning fractal for our response to the sermon, what could it look like? How could learning in the church be more like learning to ride a bike?

4. How would you divide Jesus' teaching time with the disciples and to the crowds? Let the rectangle represent all the time Jesus invested in ministry (three years). Draw a line in the box to divide it into sections for how much time he spent with the disciples and how much time he spent in public ministry like preaching and teaching. Then draw another line to represent how much our ministry invests in discipleship versus public ministry. Explain the difference. How should we be imitating Jesus' methodology?

We could be more sophisticated and ask how much time Jesus spent by himself, with his disciples alone and with his disciples in public ministry. The point is to compare this with the proportions we see practiced in the church.

5. Make a list of as many things you can think of that are influenced by social learning fractals. I have started with a few suggestions:
    a. How Canadians say 'eh' and say 'sorry' if someone else bumps into them.
    b. Different driving patterns between cultures.
    c. Unique family quirks

For personal reflection:

What is your personal learning fractal? Consider the pattern of your learning and what tends to repeat itself. How is that unique?

Chapter 3: Fractals and the Problem of Scale-up

Figure 12: Home-made pizza has been a highlight for our family for many years

When our children were growing up, we made home-made pizza on Saturday nights. It was a brilliant strategy! The kids loved it and there was always plenty of food for friends who wanted to come over. We used two huge pans, each eighteen inches across; the biggest that could fit on the two shelves of a large oven. This amount of pizza generally would leave a few leftovers for the next day for a family with three hungry teenagers. As a Dad, I loved developing the skill in making this: it was a pattern that worked so well that our children have learned to do the same today.

The design did have a problem, however, if we invited more than eight people for supper (two big slices each). The pizza took thirty minutes to bake and if we "scaled-up" by inviting sixteen people we could only feed each guest one slice in the first half hour while the second batch of pizzas were baking. We could precook some pizzas, heating them as needed. This took less time, but they tended to dry out and were not 'oven-fresh'.

A problem of scale-up

We call this a problem of scale-up; something works well on a small scale or pilot project, but as soon as the numbers increase, the very things that were attractive, must be changed in order to accommodate the crowds. We could invite more people for pizza but it would not be as good.

There are fractals that are very efficient in scaling-up. An excellent example is the online user-constructed Wikipedia. It is ten years old at the time of writing and is the fifth most popular website on the Internet. There are seventeen million articles in English (Witness, 2011) with 100,000 regular contributors who work for free adding 1,100 articles per day (Trotta, 2011). The system has been redesigned to allow massive participation which was not the case when it first started. They originally used a seven step quality-control process and it was so complicated that few contributed. But they learned the same lesson as Southwest Airlines president Herb Keller who said: "If you create an environment where people truly participate, you don't need control" (Ginsberg, Hello My Name is Blog, 2011).

Figure 13: the same Argentine bill before and after zero's were removed

Fractals can also have extremely powerful negative results on scale-up. Inflation is a negative social learning fractal. We lived in Argentina in the 1980's during a time of hyperinflation. Everyone started raising prices trying to keep ahead of the loss of purchasing power. Groceries increased in price from the time they were taken off the shelf until they were paid for. People would deposit their paycheque in term certificates of one, two and three weeks in an attempt to recover some purchasing power.

The government was continually dropping zeros from the currency. In the space of *about ten years,* this million peso bill went from having the purchasing power for two compact cars, to not being able to buy a package of gum (and six fewer zeros).

So how does scale-up happen in the church? Suppose a small discipleship group really experiences growth. The leader has high people skills; members are cared for and others are attracted. It is safe to ask questions and discussion is open. People care for each other and are significantly encouraged. Soon the house becomes crowded. The group should 'multiply' into two, four and eight groups. Sooner or later there will be a shortage of leaders and it is difficult for people to leave the comfort of being together. The lack of leadership limits additional groups being formed. Emphasis will be placed on handling more people and a large group preaching format will be used. This will require different leadership skills and the fractal changes.

Let's try to solve this problem using the family context. We normally expect everyone who wants to and is able, to care for and raise their own children. Personal care is given. Feeding is provided. Language is learned. Social skills are developed and growth occurs. Eventually children become adults and the process is repeated in the next generation. The family model scales up very effectively because the child becomes the parent and repeats the same care giving skills.

Imagine what would happen if we said: "Our pastors are paid to look after children because they are the experts. They should have the children for us. We will send our kids to their house to be fed and taught. It will be much better that way."

Two things would happen: our children wouldn't receive the continuous personal care they need and no matter how hard the pastors tried, they would burn out from the sheer magnitude of the task. Everyone would be unhappy with the results.

We get around this by finding 'super pastors' who have an exceptional teaching and preaching capacity. Their product is so good that we enjoy how the programme is scaled up. Unfortunately not all pastors can meet these expectations and they drop out[15]. At the same time, most members do not become 'spiritual parents' because they are not engaged in disciple making. Both results will eventually limit the impact in the world. There will be a shortage of really gifted preachers, a shortage of facilities big enough to hold the crowds (and the resulting debt) and the lack of mobilization that could have resulted from broad involvement of the membership.

The real tragedy is this lack of engagement of the congregants. Not having the joy of spiritual children, their contribution is marginalized and more passive. Some become bored spectators and others secretly long for a cure for their spiritual sterility. They want to be 'used of God' but there are only so many pulpits. Others who could have received spiritual nurture are left uncared for.

The desire to procreate and have offspring is very strong indeed. Yet this is something we have lost as part of our spiritual inheritance. The expectation that each family can share in the caring and nurturing of new life, has been transferred to the professional clergy. A 'structural barrenness' fractal is the pattern of expectation that the pastors have all the children and the rest of the congregation watch as spectators. The very structures we construct can work at cross purposes to reduce the disciple-making ability of the church members.

---

[15] According to Mark Elliot, "Fifteen hundred pastors leave the ministry each month and 80% of ministers feel unqualified and discouraged in their role as pastors. Eighty percent of new pastors will leave the ministry within their first five years!" (Elliot, 2009)

Church patterns for scale up

In order to handle the problem of scale-up, we can see different types of churches developing (listed in alphabetical order):

- The Ancient Church where the original paths are sought with a restoration of simplicity of worship and activities.
- The Complaining Church where no matter what the pastors are doing, they can't keep up and people feel their needs are not met. On Sunday morning the staff work as hard as they can and Monday morning the complaints start coming in. The rest of the week is used to extinguish fires. There is always the desire in the background to replace the pastor in order to find more competent staff that will produce the necessary programmes.
- The Emerging Church where change is paramount although no one knows where it will end up. It may be different from what we have now or it may morph into a new kind of traditional format.
- The Home Church where meetings at home use a small group atmosphere. It can be a 'church of small groups' where this aspect of church life is to be valued as much as Sunday attendance or as a stand-alone system of house fellowships.
- The 'Just keep faithful' Church where members demonstrate their loyalty to Christ by obediently following the system as it is. Don't rock the boat and sooner or later God will bless. The older generation are better at this brand loyalty.
- The Missional Church is where active member involvement demonstrates Christ's love by incarnating the Gospel and taking it to a hurting world.
- The Quitting Church is where people have just stopped going and quietly stay at home. Some predict these numbers are increasing (Duin, 2008).
- The Super Church where very gifted preachers can bring cohesion to the whole process: members are fed, and new staff is hired to run the programmes. There is a shortage of this type of preacher and if for some reason this preacher has to leave, the church is very vulnerable.

I need to be transparent with you. At different times I have visited or belonged to churches in each of these categories. Some I find unworkable, others unattractive and others somewhat adaptable where I can belong in community and pursue the calling to make disciples. I struggle with the feeling that the discipleship fractal seems out of synch with expectations. Efforts to make disciples are in addition to all other expectations of maintaining the programme. It is as if we make disciples in spite of the church fractal and are not empowered through the church fractal. We could argue that since we are commissioned to make disciples, the fractal should be designed around that commission. This would involve preparing a congregation to participate in experiential learning and take initiative and practice *doing* as well as *knowing*.

I want to recognize how hard people are working both employees of the religious structure and its paying members. You may be happy and the church may be growing. I am not suggesting you change anything if the system is working as you are making learners of Jesus Christ.

On the other hand, you may be extremely dissatisfied. Feelings are running high and it is not you don't care. You care very much and may have tried to promote the system, fix the system or leave the system. It is a minefield of potential conflict. I am convinced, however, that God is not in heaven wringing His hands wondering what to do. I believe in the next ten to twenty years we will see the outcomes of these options. It will be like raising children and watching what type of adults they become. It will be very interesting to observe the consequences of these design processes. I am confident that Jesus will continue to build His church as He promised.

So let´s imagine the design of a disciple-making process that can be scaled up in such a way that what the people receive in their discipleship helps them in turn to disciple others. In order to do that, we need to figure out what can't be changed in the church before we imagine what changes might occur. These essential components must be built into the DNA of the church so it becomes more self-organizing and self-reproducing.

For discussion:

1. Look at how Jesus fed the 5000. What pattern did He follow and how did this permit scaling up? (Mark 6:34-44)
2. Draw a 'rich picture' of your faith community. (A rich picture is a diagram that captures as many components of how things really work. Use icons, arrows, labels or images to capture ideas and feelings. Include how your church 'scales-up' and how discipleship is carried out. You may wish to draw it from the perspective of a member of the congregation or as a leader depending on your role. Consider how your life as a disciple interfaces with the system. See definition[16] of rich picture and a tutorial[17]
3. Identify other church scale-up patterns if not listed above. What are the fractal patterns you observe?
4. Discuss this case study based on a true story:

A man starts an outreach Bible study in his neighbourhood and soon close to forty people are attending. His pastor feels that this now should be run in a more traditional church format and wants to take over the leadership of the group and he runs it like a church service. Attendance drops to three or four people. The original leader takes over again and attendance rebounds to the larger size. Then the pastor takes over and the attendance drops again. How does this illustrate a scale-up problem? Propose a fractal solution.

For personal reflection:

How important to you is scaling-up the blessing you are receiving from Jesus to the whole world?

[16] http://en.wikipedia.org/wiki/Rich_picture
[17] http://systems.open.ac.uk/materials/T552/

Section 2: A Discipleship Fractal

Lee Iacocca said "The main thing is to keep the main thing the main thing." It was great advice for the Chrysler Corporation which was facing bankruptcy at the time. Part of pattern recognition is to identify what parts of the pattern are essential and what can be changed and adapted. In this section we will look at the unchanging elements of the discipleship fractal which include:

- Chapter 4: The Jesus Kernel
- Chapter 5: A Discipleship Cycle

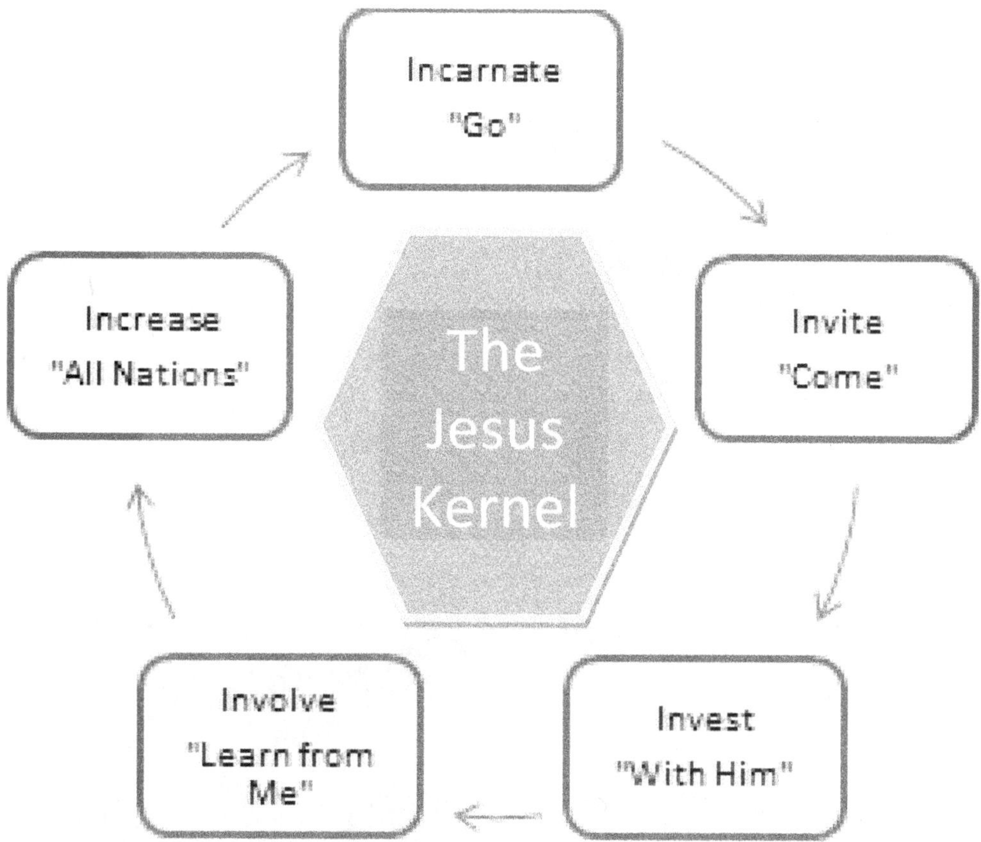

Figure 14: A Discipleship Fractal

Chapter 4: The Jesus Kernel

Most of us have one time or another commented on the Microsoft Windows® operating system for personal computers. Some of us have chosen Mac® computers (and not letting the rest of us forget it) while the remainder sticks with their PCs. [18]

But there is another story of the Linux® open source operating system. Anyone can get the programming code for free, develop it and share it to be tested and improved. Thousands are investing their time and skills in producing an operating system that is now being used on the ten fastest computers in the world (Burkhardt, 2010) and on the majority of the servers.

I love the title of a chapter in the book, *The Cathedral and the Bazaar,* called "How many eyeballs tame complexity" (Raymond, 2000). In this story of Linux, the idea is that many contributors in an open-sharing, free, motivational environment will find better solutions than what can be obtained from fewer contributors in a highly controlled, top-down, paid group. Many eyeballs can tame complexity.

Linux uses a concept called *the kernel*. You can change anything or add anything you want in the thousands of lines of computer code but you can't touch the kernel. This is the part that makes everything else work. It is a brilliant design strategy of extreme flexibility for most things and extreme rigidity for a very few things. Do you see the fractal here? This design parameter has enabled it to scale up immensely.

We can think of the 'kernel' as the nucleus. In living cells, it contains the DNA so that every time the cell divides, it makes an exact replica of its genetic material. All the instructions are there and scale-up is integrated in the design.

What kernel fractal do we use in the church? This is a trick question. If you listened to many complaints you would think that at best we have constructed a very large and unmanageable kernel of "change at your peril". Just try changing something and you will find out if it is in the kernel or not. The story is told of the pastor who wanted to move the piano from one side of the pulpit to the other, so he moved it a few inches every week until he got it where he wanted. He managed to slip it by the "change police" and averted a crisis.

The *bloated kernel* creates another problem. When we become swamped by change, the risk is high that the few things that shouldn't change get blown away along with everything else. The fractal of the nucleus suggests that we identify the smallest selection possible of absolute unchangeable principles. Then we need to be extremely flexible with everything else in order to learn, change, adapt and improve according to local needs and global priorities.[19]

---

[18] Used with permission http://www.microsoft.com/About/Legal/EN/US/IntellectualProperty/Permissions/Default.aspx Mac is a trademark of Apple. Inc http://www.apple.com/legal/trademark/guidelinesfor3rdparties.html Linux is a trademark of the Linux Foundation. http://www.linuxfoundation.org/about/linux-foundation-trademark-usage-guidelines

[19] This is assuming healthy cell reproduction according to the DNA and not cancer.

The Jesus kernel

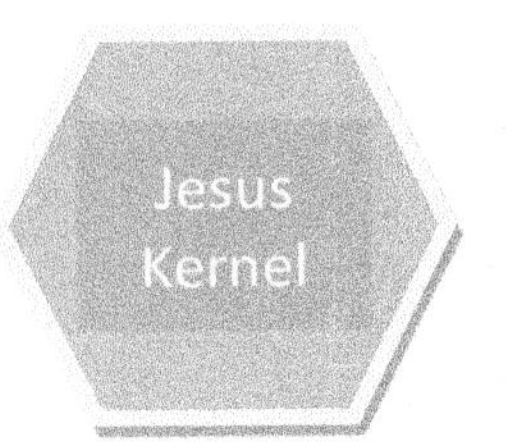

Let me suggest in broad strokes what could be included in the Jesus' kernel that is completely compatible with scale-up in design for the church:

- Relationship with God through Jesus Christ as Word and Spirit
- Our response of faith and obedience to His commands
- Loving community and reaching out to the world.[20]

We cannot emphasize the centrality of Christ enough: "The Word became flesh and dwelt among us and we beheld His glory, the glory as of the only begotten from the Father, full of grace and truth."[21] His work on the cross and what constitutes salvation is inseparable.[22] The Holy Spirit as teacher and the life-changing interaction with His community cannot be minimized. The kernel is serious business and we need to be careful neither to add to it nor take away from this core teaching.[23] At the same time I recognize how we express this has some variance in interpretation. It is not my intention to debate the differences of what to be included or not. We are all called to be learners of the core teaching of the Gospel. The kernel's role in the fractal is that it does not change no matter what else happens and it faithfully reproduces itself on scale-up.

Someone said that the Gospel is so simple that it is like a river shallow enough that even the smallest child can play safely but so deep that even the greatest theologian cannot touch the bottom. If the Kingdom of heaven belongs to the children,[24] then we must keep the kernel simple[25].

I remember when I first encountered the Gospel. To understand what it meant that Jesus loved me and died for me on the cross was amazing. It was so transformational that a few years later I found a letter I had written to a family member before really understanding the Gospel. I described how life was just a joke not worth living. It was so negative that I never even mailed the letter. The funny thing was that although I recognized my hand writing I had forgotten the desperation I had been living and realized how the Lord restored joy in my life.

The kernel is all about the pearl of great price[26] which when found, we 'sell all' in response to the treasure we have in Jesus. Jesus rightfully has first place in everything (pre-eminence) where everything

---

[20] This is summarized in The Wheel illustration of The Navigators: http://www.navigators.org/us/resources/illustrations/items/the_wheel
[21] John 1:14
[22] John 1:12
[23] Revelations 22:18, 19
[24] Matt. 19:14
[25] My kids tell me I can "nerdify" anything. Give me something simple and somehow I can make it complicated. There have been times they have asked me a question and then quickly caught themselves and said, "Dad, if you are going to make this really complicated then I don't want to know".

[26] Matt. 13:45,46

is summed up in Him.[27] As learners we start with Jesus since in Him is hidden all the treasures of wisdom and knowledge[28]. As we learn what He is like and the vastness of his resources, we begin to understand the various aspects of our needs and how these are met as we learn from Him.

Perhaps the briefest summary of the kernel is the declaration" Jesus is Lord". While the Scriptures affirm no one can say Jesus is Lord except by the Spirit of God (1 Corinthians 12:3) we also know that many will say "Lord, Lord" and who do not know God. (Matthew 7:21-23) This suggests that there is no infallible litmus test and we are going to have to live with the fact that the Lord" knows those who are His" (2 Timothy 2:19). The early church participants identified each other by drawing two strokes on the ground forming the figure of a fish. The Greek word for Fish (ΙΧΘΥΣ) was an acronym for the title *Jesus Christ, God's Son, Savior.* This suggests adequate parameters for the kernel.

He invites us to follow Him unconditionally where we are prepared to pay a cost of cross-bearing and self-denial. It doesn't mean that it is the first and only thing we talk about but it is like our genetic code, forming who we are and guiding us in all we do. Before we continue seeing how Jesus addressed the problem of "scaling up" in making disciples, we need to be sure we have the kernel clear in our thinking.

For discussion:

1. What should be included in the DNA of the Kernel?
2. Can you remember what attracted you to Jesus? What Good News do people see in your life?
3. Where are we in danger of losing or changing the kernel today? Reflect on your understanding of the Jesus kernel and whether it is being reflected in everything you do.

For personal reflection:

Look at the message of your faith community and what is being passed on as the fractal that reproduces itself. What would visitors, members, pastoral staff say is the nucleus?

[27] Eph 1:10, Col 2:9,10
[28] Col 2:3

Chapter 5: A Discipleship Cycle

Figure 15: Jim (L) and John (R) are standing beside their Dad. Each is imitating the way he stands.

No one taught these twin boys how to stand beside their dad. If Dad has his hands in his pocket, Jim had his hands that way. If Dad had his hands behind his back, John had his hands that way. No one asked them to stand this way or told them to imitate whatever Dad was doing. Why did they do this without being told?

Have you ever met the children of a friend whom you have not seen for twenty years? The young adult comes to the door and you think this is a miniature version of your friend. Why does this happen?

The answer to these questions is that we learn almost everything by imitation, from family life to discipleship. It is the key to understanding the social learning fractal. This universal trait is very significant in the method Jesus used to make disciples and one we need to learn to imitate[29].

Jesus used a five step fractal in the discipling process:

---

[29] "Imitation" can be used either as a cheap fake replica of something of value or the process of learning to be like the other. Obviously I am using the second meaning here. I also realize that Jesus' incarnation meant that God took human form. Our incarnation is more like crossing cultural barriers and comfort zones.

- He entered into the world of those He was reaching (Incarnate)
- He reached out to people inviting then to come follow Him in order to be learners of Him (Invite)
- He intentionally developed a close life-relationship with His disciples (Invest)
- He assigned them progressively more difficult tasks so they could learn by doing (Involve)
- He sent them off to repeat the process to the point of including all nations (Increase)

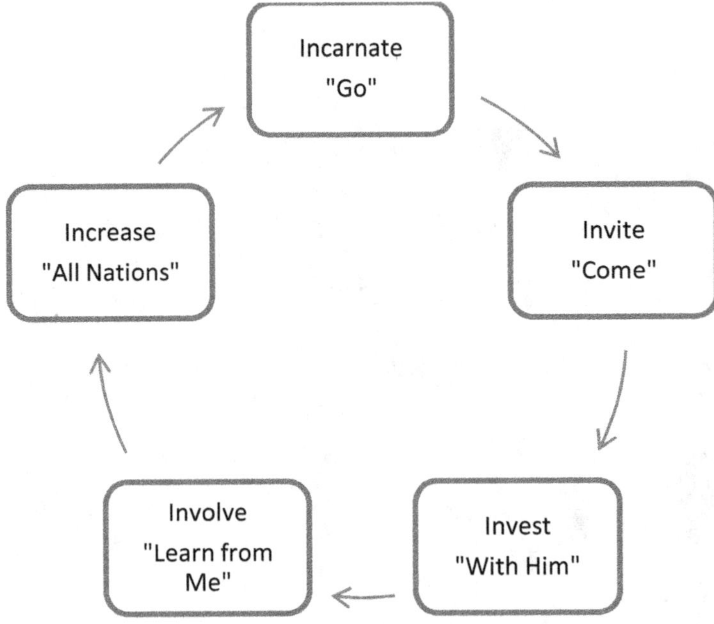

Figure 16; Five Step Disciple-Making Fractal

He began by entering into the world of those He wanted to reach. He spent thirty years in preparation as a family member and carpenter. The Word became flesh (incarnate) and "dwelt among us".[30] In the Message it says the Word "moved into our neighbourhood". This meant learning to like what people like: their food, their music, the way they dress, the things they do to be friends.

Then He purposefully invited certain people to come follow Him[31] and shared a more purposeful relationship where He gave time and attention to help them grow. They were free to respond by accepting or not. It was not forced or manipulative. It was something they wanted to do.

His strategy was for them to be *with Him*.[32] This 'with Him' principle is like being real family, where there is a familiarity, constancy and an involvement in people's lives. It had such a profound effect on the disciples. [33]

[30] John 1:14
[31] Matthew 4:19
[32] Mark 3:14
[33] Gord Jones calls this kind of relationship a *hyphenated reality*, where *Gord* and *Jim* is different that *Gord-Jim*.

Even the opponents of the Gospel recognized that these unlearned fishermen had 'been with' Jesus.[34] Something rubbed off from that three year time together that was very Jesus-like: their boldness and confidence in God, their ability to challenge the system and the way they prayed.

He involved them in ministry assignments to try, fail, question, reflect and learn. This was an experiential learning model where the disciples were expected to 'do' and not just 'know'. They failed, questioned their teacher and were questioned, observed Him, received additional explanations and accompanied Jesus wherever he went. The lessons became progressively more challenging beginning with watching Jesus, then imitating His ministry while he watched, from short assignments and reporting back to a life-long calling. They were sent out to 'go' and live out the same strategy with others.[35]

Paul imitated this method in developing father/mother discipleship relationships to the Gentile believers, calling Timothy his own 'son' and being confident of having shared all aspects of his life and teaching with him. He also charged Timothy to take all that he had learned from Paul and "entrust to faithful people who can teach others also". [36]

In examples of Jesus and Paul we see a fractal process which can scale up to any size. Because this is to be passed on as it was received, it can continually increase in scale without losing effectiveness.

However the pattern starts slowly and we are tempted to look for a quick fix. As a pastor, I have tried to demonstrate the 'with him' fractal to the whole congregation but it doesn't work. It is one-way communication. I can talk to them but I don't hear their stories. Five or six at the dinner table is a family. Two hundred or three hundred regularly at a table is an orphanage or a community feeding centre. We need to figure how to scale-up the 'with Him" fractal in a different way than just preaching to them.

Multiplication as a fractal process

For sake of argument, suppose it took Jesus three years to make eleven disciples[37] and each disciple in turn took three years to do the same. Mathematical progressions are dehumanizing but let's use it to illustrate a point. We calculate the growth of the number of disciples over a period of twenty-four years if every disciple produced eleven disciples every three years:

1. 11 disciples by year 3
2. 121 disciples by year 6
3. 1331 disciples by year 9 (This is still pretty slow after a decade of work!)
4. 14,641 disciples by year 12
5. 161,051 disciples by year 15
6. 1,771,561 disciples by year 18
7. 19,487,171 disciples by year 21

---

[34] Acts 4:13

[35] Matthew 28:18-20

[36] 1Thes 2:7-11; 2 Timothy 2:1; 2Timothy 3:10,11; 2Timothy 2:2

[37] We will leave out Judas and while we know Matthias was added, there could have been other disciples not mentioned. We should note that Jesus had a retention issue with Judas.

8. 214,358,881 disciples by year 24 (approaching the world population at that time)

So if this is a 'biblical fractal', did the world become Christian in a generation? There are some intriguing verses to that suggest while not all became Christian, that 'the message sounded forth in every place" so that there was no more need for Paul to say anything[38] and that "the faith had been proclaimed through the whole world".[39] This would be a dream come true for our world today.

We know that not all the apostles lived for twenty-four years after Christ's death so the mathematical sequence is purely theoretical. According to Acts 12:1, 2 James, the son of Zebedee was martyred by Herod Agrippa about eleven years after Jesus' death and resurrection. We don't know if all the disciples had the same number of talents or if their seeds multiplied at the same rate (30, 60 and 100 fold). I don't think the Kingdom of God progresses in a purely geometrical fashion and God is not limited by a mathematical model. Nevertheless, the results are astounding when the "with Him" fractal 'multiplies' eight times (recursions) to reach the population of the world at that time.

Parents and grandparents

To understand the power and cost of the "with Him" fractal, think about what do you need to do in order to become a parent and properly raise children?[40] We can imagine the cost in time, effort and commitment. We call this step *reproduction* (or spiritual reproduction for discipleship).

What do you have to do to become a grandparent? We really can't do anything. It will happen on its own time. We call this step *(spiritual) multiplication*". Parents invest a great deal in order to raise a family but multiplication will happen on its own and as grandparents, we can't really do anything about it. This is captured in the fractal where each generation invests "being with" their children in the reproduction stage and then watching the multiplication stage happen in the stages of grandchildren and beyond.

I can't begin to describe our joy in seeing our three children as adults along with each of their spouses. Raising them has been a twenty-five year investment but infinitely worth it. Now and in the coming years they will form their own families and we will cheer them on the best we can. Naomi and I reproduced ourselves by having three children. Now we are at the multiplication stage with one granddaughter and someday perhaps more. We glimpse a cycle that has repeated itself generation after generation.

This also happens spiritually. I remember years ago when I worked in student ministry helping Clive learn to share his faith and help young believers grow. We spent a lot of time together in a 'with him' relationship. God blessed Clive and he led Charlie to the Lord and spent significant time 'with him'. Charlie grew in his faith and eventually went to be a missionary in Vietnam. Charlie and his family have wonderful stories of 'with him' relationships with the people there. God, by His grace, blessed in

---

[38] 1Thes. 1:8

[39] Romans 1:8

[40] I am grateful to Alan Middleton of Dynamic Churches International for this insight.

reproducing my spiritual walk in Clive, it was multiplied in Charlie and continues to multiply in people I expect to meet one day in heaven.

For discussion:

1. What have you learned by imitation in your Christian life? Both good and bad?
2. Can you think of more illustrations from the Gospels of the Jesus "with Him" fractal?
3. Who is imitating you in the way you are a disciple? Compare and contrast with the discipleship pattern you received?
4. How is the discipleship cycle similar to the way a nucleus divides reproducing the genetic code?

For personal reflection:

What is the fractal pattern in your faith community how people relate to friends and new comers?

Section 3: Divine Resources

Figure 17: Prayer and the Scriptures are like parallel track for a train

An absolutely necessary part of the discipleship fractal is how to access the resources from God in order to make disciples. There are different ways that this could be described but we can think of a conversation, where God speaks to us through the Scriptures and we respond in prayer. The Holy Spirit is the agent in communicating with our hearts. In this section we will look at:

- Chapter 6: Promise Claiming
- Chapter 7: Scripture Resources
- Chapter 8: Prayer Resources

Chapter 6: Promise Claiming

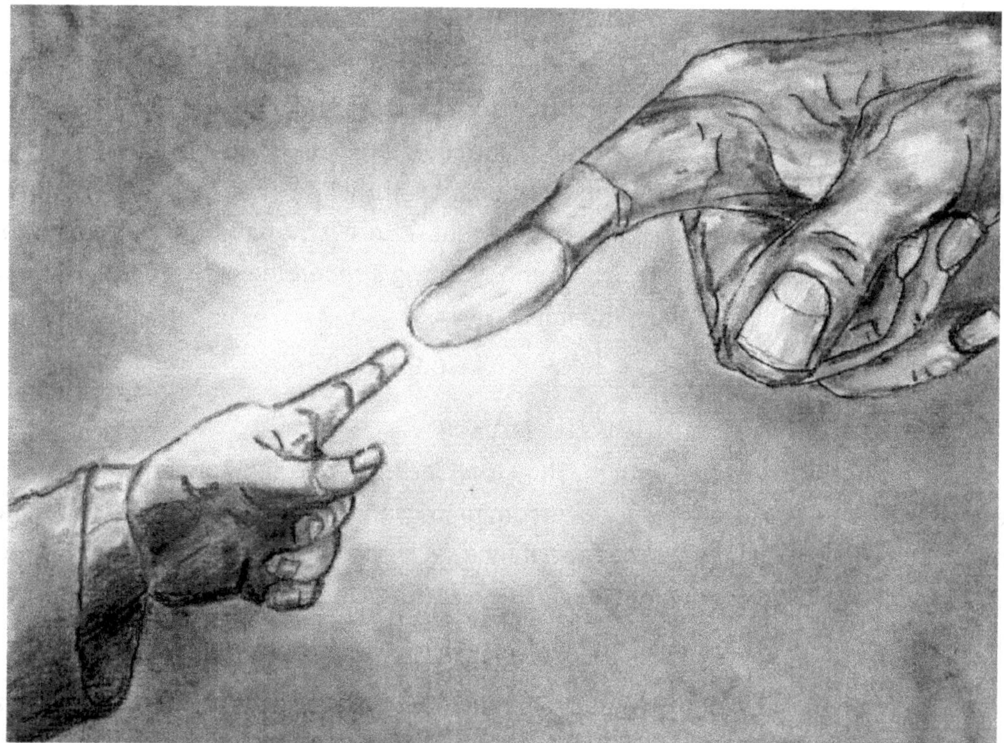

Figure 18: Trustworthy Promises

I remember as a young Christian I struggled with feeling that I was never going to be much use to God. I didn't know enough. I didn't have a flashy personality. It seemed to me that just living life was a challenge. But somehow I was encouraged that God uses ordinary people and so I volunteered. "Whatever you want, Lord, please help me be available and willing." I have probably given up on that prayer a 1000 times in the last thirty-seven years only to come back to God again and again and say "yes Lord, that is what I want".

Somewhere I was pointed to the promises in the Bible as the starting place for weak people to find the supernatural strength they needed. I was encouraged to take these precious and magnificent promises,[41] carefully observe any necessary conditions and simply ask God to fulfill His intentions according to Christ's merit and by the power of the Holy Spirit. I found myself praying really quite outrageous things like, "Lord, I would like a spiritual inheritance that reaches the nations of the world." Some of these promises have the dates Oct 6, 1974, Jan 6, 1976 and March 24, 1977 which I have written in the margins of the Bible I use. When I leaf through it I remember those moments when I decided to boldly ask God to do what I could never do.

---

[41] 2 Peter 1:3-4

When I look back I am astounded. Not that I even expect to see all of the blessings before I get to heaven, but the ones I do see leave me speechless. "Lord, Your promises really are precious and magnificent."

Jesus and promise claiming

Is claiming promises from the Scriptures a repeating pattern observed in Jesus' ministry? This question merits an in depth study[42]. Jesus was aware of promises relating to how He and John the Baptist fulfilled Scripture,[43] His own unique Lordship, the rejection, unbelief, family conflict, misunderstanding of parables, betrayal, death and resurrection and triumphant return. The early church taught the promises were to be passed down from parents to children and that we are joint heirs with Christ of the promises. Promises guided the Lord and the early church demonstrating a repeating pattern of trusting what was promised. We call this a "promise-claiming fractal".

Inheritance promises and making disciples

What do claiming promises have to do with making disciples? The promise concerns receiving a spiritual inheritance or in Biblical terms, promises for overcoming barrenness: the condition of not being able to have children.[44] Barrenness will prevent the inheritance of the promise from one generation to another and barrenness in making disciples prevents receiving a spiritual inheritance of the blessing of future generations.

After the amazing prophetic view of the Messiah in Isaiah 53, the very next words are "Shout for joy, O barren one, you who have borne no child." Bareness is a very sad condition. To be barren at that time was to forfeit your value as a person.

The suffering of those who cannot have children is intense. To be asked to rejoice in this condition seems insensitive and cruel nevertheless this promises that the number of offspring to the desolate will be greater than for those with children. The barren are encouraged to "enlarge the place of [their] tent". While this concept has been used to support countless church building projects, I think it refers to the family tent: the place where the barren family will have their offspring. In other words, 'get the crib ready and prepare the nursery'.

The reason to do this is given: "For your husband is your maker, whose name is the Lord of Hosts" (verse 5). The fractal pattern is that with God's enabling, we all can have many offspring, take care of them and see them multiply to the next generation.

This promise is repeated in a number of passages including:

---

[42] The NASB Study Bible (Lockman Foundation) uses an uppercase font to indicate Old Testament passages quoted in the New Testament and makes it quite visual to see what promises Jesus referred to.

[43] Luke 4: 16-21; 7:24-28; Luke 20:41-44; Luke 20:17; John 12:38-40; Matthew 10:35,36; Mark 4:11,12; Matthew 16:21; Psalm 16:10; John 13:18; Matthew 26:64; Acts 13:32-35; Galatians 3:29

[44] I will not differentiate between physical children and spiritual descendants as it is God's power which gives both.

- "The smallest one will become a clan and the least one a mighty nation" (Isaiah 60:22).
- "Ask of me and I will give the nations as your inheritance, the very ends of the earth as your possession" (Psalm 2:8).

The conditions for the fulfillment of the promise of descendants are fully met in Jesus, His work on the Cross and His divine authority. We are joint heirs of these benefits when we trust in Him. In fact all the promises in the Bible are 'Yes and Amen" in Jesus.[45] He is the master qualifier for all things promised in the Scriptures.

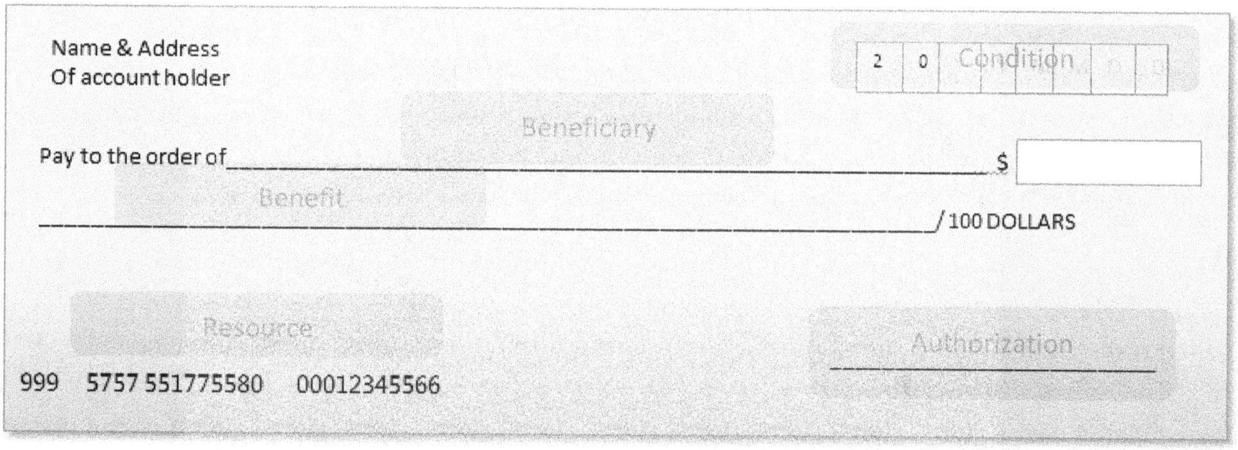

Name & Address
Of account holder

2 0 Condition

Beneficiary

Pay to the order of ______ $

Benefit

______ /100 DOLLARS

Resource

Authorization

999 5757 551775580 00012345566

Figure 19: A cheque is a type of promise.

A bank cheque is a type of promise which we can use to understand these components. There is a beneficiary who will receive a benefit of a certain value which is authorized by the owner of certain resources. It is subject to certain conditions such as a time frame and proof of identity. We can analyze all promises according to this rubric. There is an exercise at the end of the chapter matching these components with some promises in the Bible.

The idea of authorization of the promise was brought home forcible to me a few years ago. I was alone in the house and it was about 6 am. I was just in between being asleep and being awake. I heard the word 'Yes' and I sat bolt upright in bed. My first reaction was "That voice needs to be obeyed!" It sounded like the Ancient of Days. Nothing happened after that and I got up a little shaken and started my day. Later I went to a prayer meeting. The other pastor opened his Bible and read 2 Corinthians 1:20; "For no matter how many promises God has made, they are "Yes" in Christ. And so through him the "Amen" is spoken by us to the glory of God".

I felt the colour drain from my face as he read this verse. "I have to tell you what happened to me this morning" I told him. "I cannot explain if the 'Yes' I heard was a dream or a vision, but I do know it impressed upon me that it is Jesus who says 'Yes' over his promises and he wants to give spiritual descendants to all his children." The "yes of Jesus" is sufficient for the scale-up necessary to give a spiritual inheritance to all His children and to reach the whole world.

[45] 2 Corinthians 1:20

God has driven this lesson home to me in another unique way. I have had many opportunities to pray for people who are trying to have children. In travelling around Latin America, I have had mothers come up to me on a return visit bouncing a little baby and saying "Pastor, look what you have done!" I am quick to make it clear that God has done this according to His promises and that my role was rather indirect of simply praying. (They never meant it any other way but I love pointing people to the greatness of the promises.)

The "promises claiming fractal" is quite exciting. God's promises can never be used up, they can never wear out and they can scale-up to any size necessary. When I trust God for what He promises and then our children trust God, using the same promises and their children after them, in no way do these promises run out of gas. Jesus said "Heaven and earth will pass away but my words will never pass away.[46] The words of God will not return to heaven without accomplishing His desire.[47] They are as much a hammer, fire and sword today and will be tomorrow as they were in ages past.

It is also exciting because God takes into full account that we are weak. In fact God seems to take particular delight in blessing the weak.[48] So if I am without an ounce of strength, the promises of God are still completely trustworthy for all God wants to do in and through me and these promises will still be there for the generations that follow. What was first given to Abraham and through Christ is available for everyone who trusts in Him. The descendants can be as numerous as the stars of heaven[49] and the promises will still work. They will work for anybody anywhere as long as we are trusting in Christ. I don't have to do the ministry in my own strength. [50]

Promises are based on Jesus' work on the cross. His victory over death and ascension into heaven enables the promises to have power! As great High Priest he offered Himself as the sacrificial Lamb satisfying the justice of God for our sins.[51] He lives to make intercession for us.[52] The verse before that, describes his Word as a two edged sword that cuts and lays open our hearts and in Revelation we see Him with the sword coming from his mouth.[53] Promises have authority and are the blueprints for Jesus' ministry.

---

[46] Mark 13:31
[47] Isaiah 55:11
[48] 1 Corinthians 1:26-31
[49] Genesis 15:5
[50] I do not mean to minimize at all those who suffer from continued physical barrenness, who have prayed and trusted the promises of God. Some couples have spent thousands of dollars in treatments, sought international adoption and remain disappointed. This pain is real. God may have a different type of inheritance in mind for these promises to be fulfilled. In giving ourselves to the hungry of this world (physical, emotional spiritual) He can surround us with 'adopted spiritual children' who will treasure the love and care we give. There is no shortage of people like this.

[51] Hebrews 7:25-28
[52] Hebrews 4:13, 14
[53] Revelation 1:16

Here are two words of caution about promises in the Bible. We do need to be careful not to see the Bible as a "Promises" supermarket where we can consume the promises of our choosing. We must not only be hearing the Word and seeking its' benefits but also be putting it into action.[54] It is like the problem of obesity today in Western society where we are consuming more nutrients than we are utilizing. We are becoming spiritual couch potatoes. Rather we should be using what we have taken in the Scripture through listening to sermons, reading, study, memorizing and meditation for personal transformed and for a blessing to others.

Secondly, claiming promises is not a fast track to an easy inheritance. Although it took Jesus 3 years to make this kind of investment in his disciples, we want to do make disciples in three weeks or three hours. We want to turbo drive the training to get the maximum amount of information transfer as quickly as possible. This may work for some issues requiring information but we risk not properly caring for that first generation. They can only imitate what they have seen and they won't know how to multiply.

Promise claiming involves:

- Identifying the conditions of the promise. Some promises are entirely based on Christ's actions while other promises have a component that the individual must fulfill.[55]
- If those conditions are met, then claim the promise. Faith pleases God[56] so ask boldly.[57]
- Review the promise often. I like to write the date in the margin of the Bible. This has been a great source of encouragement as I come across them in my reading or when I am seeking God for guidance.

We start with the Promises of God because we must start with His resources. Discipleship is not a matter of tweaking the current system to get better preachers or more training for small group leaders. It is not a programme based on good planning and strategy. Only the Promises have the power to scale up to the size necessary for blessing the whole world. Generation after generation can follow the promise-claiming fractal to receive an inheritance of the nations.

Today when politicians and religious leaders seem to be continually 'spinning' the truth and covering up their plans, the whole idea of being able to trust God's promises seems unbelievable. Yet He can be trusted for fruitfulness to have spiritual descendants. Ask Him. He invites you to.

For discussion:

1. Read Isaiah 54 and note what stands out. Can we claim this promise for ourselves? Why or why not?

---

[54] James 1:22
[55] Compare Ephesians 1:3 with Psalm 2:8.
[56] Hebrews 11:6
[57] Hebrews 4:16

2. How is promise claiming like a fractal that can handle any scale? What short cuts, quicker or less costly solutions do we seek instead of claiming the promises for an inheritance?
3. What promises from the Scriptures are important to you? What are you asking from God? How have you seen that fulfilled? Where are you still waiting and what is that experience like?
4. How does the cross relate to the Promises of God? What is Jesus' role in the promises in the past, present and future?
5. I have always liked to put dates beside promises that I have felt prompted to claim for different circumstances. Have you ever done that? Are there any results you would like to share with others?
6. In the website discussion forum there is a chart to fill in with promises from the Scriptures and an analysis of their components. (See introduction for access to the discussion forum.)

For personal reflection:

What are the observable evidences of God's promises being the foundation of faith and action in your faith community? How is "promise claiming" being built into the fractal from new believers to mature labourers so that they are encouraged to rely on God's resources?

Chapter 7: Scripture Resources

Figure 20: Training wheels for young believers

Tim (our middle child) as a baby had a stomach upset while he was still "on the bottle". He was not supposed to drink milk for a couple of days. At the same time Naomi had to go to a conference for the weekend and I was left in charge of all things related to feeding. No matter what I tried, no liquids were acceptable to him and so I decided to mix the smallest amount of formula powder just to colour the liquid white. When he saw the bottle, his face lit up. He took a big gulp but reacted with disgust. It looked like milk but it didn't taste like it!

I have often thought of that with the verse "Like newborn babes, long for the pure milk of the Word".[58] In Tim's case, he quickly recognized that it was not pure milk he was given and he knew the difference.

In this chapter, I want to present ideas of what can be done with 'just the Bible'. I am not against Bible study materials which certainly have their role to help people grow. But I am thinking of some things that can be as available as mother's milk; the type of things you can help another Christian grow as you meet for a coffee and a 45 minute visit.

"Seven Minutes with God"

Do you know a newborn has a stomach the size of a shooter marble? (Mohrbacher) No wonder the baby needs to drink just a little bit of milk every couple of hours! A baby can get sick from eating too much,

[58] 1 Peter2:2

too fast. In the same way, a new born Christian requires small frequent meals from the Scriptures rather than huge eat-fests separated by large intervals.

"Seven Minutes with God" is a five step process that you can write on a napkin or number on the fingers of one hand as you meet with a new Christian.

1. Pray and ask God to speak to me.
2. Read a paragraph or chapter of the Bible (starting in one of the Gospels or a Psalm)
3. Reread it
4. Pick a favorite verse.
5. Pray and ask God to use this truth in my life.

I like to share Mark 1:35 as to why this devotional time is important. "Very early in the morning, while it was still dark, Jesus got up, left the house and went off to a solitary place, where he prayed." I also discuss why this is such an important part of my life. Psalm 1 is a good place for practicing together. The most important step is to DO IT TOGETHER.

Later on variations can be introduced:

- Start the weekly Bible study by asking people to share highlights from their time with God throughout the week. (Rather than take the time for everybody to share with everybody, divide into 2's or 3's to share together.)
- Encourage people to write in a journal or notebook their favorite verse and why is it is important.
- Review the devotional journal and highlight significant thoughts to summarize what God has been saying over time.
- Remind people that the way they have learned to develop their devotional life, they can repeat with others. (Establish the fractal).
- Talk about what you get from your devotional time. If you have trouble being regular at this, try establishing a special spot and routine where you go and meet with God.
- Use the Lectio Divina[59] or imagining techniques to place yourself in the passage and observe what you are thinking and feeling as you see the events unfold.

'Listening to God's voice' is the foundation on which all other growth occurs. It is just like milk to a baby. Can you imagine what would happen in a church if the whole congregation would daily have an open heart to listen to His word? I believe it would be worthwhile ministry just to teach this practical tool to others in such a way that they could teach others. Whenever I teach this tool face-to-face we practice it together.

It is important to understand that these are starting steps, like the training wheels on a bike (figure 20). They are meant to be removed for the bike to really be used as it was designed. Similarly 'Seven Minutes

[59] See http://en.wikipedia.org/wiki/Lectio_Divina

with God' is 'a simple plan for a small stomach' and is meant to be outgrown. This will feel quite restrictive if carried on in such a scripted fashion but is very effective to begin the journey.

We can actually teach many skills as a simple follow-up plan in this 'experiential format'. It does not require anything complicated and serves as an idea for your time together:

- Tell your STORY on how you personally experience this skill or understanding about God
- Look at a key VERSE from the Scriptures that teaches the truth
- Explain a simple ACTIVITY that helps practice the experience
- Do this activity TOGETHER

Bible study on a page

I do dream of people in the church being able to invest an hour of personal preparation of a Bible passage as opposed to being restricted to only receiving insights from being told from someone else's sermon. As I mentioned before, I am not against sermons, but if the flock can learn to feed themselves, then pastors are more available to concentrate on equipping the saints for the work of service (Ephesian 4:12).

Inductive Bible study uses three steps:

- Observation: what does it say
- Interpretation: what does it mean
- Application: what action should be taken based on this passage

There are a number of methods that can be used but the important thing is to get into the Scriptures, prayerfully observe, chew over the content and seek to put it into practice. Irving Jensen's book *Independent Bible Study* is a real treasure if you can find it. "If you want to own just one book on this subject this is the one to get!" (Eriksson, 2000)

Jensen's central idea is to copy the passage 'as is' except that you introduce spaces in order to display the argument. The best way to explain this is to demonstrate this from Hebrews 4:12. Observe how the passage reads the same in spite of the spaces added.

For the word of God
        is   alive and active.
                    Sharper than any double-edged sword,
  it *penetrates* even to dividing
                    soul and spirit,
                    joints and marrow;
  It *judges* the thoughts and attitudes of the heart.

Figure 21: Example of how to position text on the page.

Look at what stands out. Can you see the three verbs? The Word of God *is* and *does* (penetrates and discerns). We observe varied characteristics of what it is and how it works. There are a number of pairs that are identified and can be compared. We can then interpret what this means and work toward an application.

Writing out the passage in this way (or copy/paste it in a word processor and then add spaces) is a powerful meditation technique. You could add different fonts or colours and additional columns on each side of the page for cross references and an outline. There are other Bible study methods like topical, character, historical background and it is worth the effort to develop these skills. Find someone who demonstrates skill in studying the Scriptures and ask them to mentor you.

The plural *'you* '

I have spent years learning Spanish and an added bonus has been reading the Bible in a language other than English. This has really challenged some of my interpretations. It centers on the word *'you'*. In many languages there is *you* (singular) and *you* (plural) but in English we use the same word for both. Now consider the following verse and think about whether it is *you* singular or *you* plural.

"If you continue in my word you will know the truth and the truth will set you free". [60]

I had always felt that it meant that if *I* (singular) continued in the Word then *I* (singular) would be freed by truth. I was shocked to find out that this passage uses *you* (plural). My paraphrase of this verse is "If *you all continue together* in the word then *you all together* will be liberated by truth". In other words, there is a community life in the Word, where we all must continue in the Scriptures (with implied interaction, correction and mutual guidance) in order to receive the promised benefit. It is not enough that I have my personal quiet time. This challenges my North American independent paradigm[61].

Bible study facilitator

Here are some brief suggestions for leading Bible discussions.

1. Pattern the questions you ask on the inductive sequence. I'll demonstrate it using an example:
    - What stood out to you in the Jesus' words of John 8:31, 32? (Observation)
    - What does it mean when Jesus said "if you continue in My word"? (Interpretation)
    - How do you feel challenged to do that this week? What new skills do you need in order to do that? (Application)
2. Don't use questions that can be answered *yes* or *no* because it will not produce discussion. Consider the difference between the two questions for generating discussion:
    - Is it important to read the Bible?
    - Why is it important to read the Bible?

---

[60] John 8:31,32

[61] Curiously the King James gives us clues to *you* (singular) and *you* (plural) by using *thou/thee (singular)* and *ye/you (plural). The two forms are for subject* or object in the sentence.

3. When asking questions, give time for people to think or else you will get nervous, answer your own question and the discussion dies. If no one responds, ask "Did you understand the question?"

After someone answers a question instead of asking another one or commenting on every answer, ask others, "What do others think?" This is especially important if the answer is wrong or incomplete.

Consider what the Bible says of itself. The Word of God is more desirable than gold and sweeter than honey; it is a lamp to our feet and light on our path. It will not pass away and endures forever; it is a devouring flame, a crushing hammer and a defensive weapon. This Word can be joy and delight but sometimes it is hard on the stomach. It is worth the effort to become skilled in handling the Word and being able to teach others as well.[62]

For discussion:

1. There are several warnings against hearing His voice and hardening your heart (Hebrews 3:7, 15; 4:7; Psalm 95:7, 8). How can we encourage one another not to do that?
2. What would a church look like if everyone was actively listening to God and teaching others to do the same? How would the pastor's role change?
3. Use the STORY/VERSE/TOOL/TOGETHER plan to design a follow-up tool to teach some aspect of discipleship.
4. Practice leading a small group discussion and ask for suggestions on how to do it better.
5. Practice journaling. How have you found that experience?
6. What Bible study methods have you tried and what is most useful. Compare methods.
7. Evaluate whether you consider yourself a skilled worker in the Word? What could you do to change that?
8. An additional resource is included in Appendix A can be photocopied and used as a handout for beginner Bible studies.

For personal reflection:

As a community, how is the Word of God shaping your beliefs, actions and lives? Is the fractal approach self-organizing, expansive and empowering to every individual, just as learning to ride a bike permits you to ride anywhere?

[62] Psalm 19:10; Psalm 119:105; Matthew 24:35; 1Peter 1:25; Jeremiah 5:14; Jeremiah 23:29; Ephesians 6:17; Jeremiah 15:16; Revelation 10:10; 2 Timothy 2:15

Chapter 8: Prayer Resources

The first time I ever went to a small group Bible study was at university and the first time I showed up was a supper meeting and they asked me to say grace. I had never prayed out loud (other than the standard prayers) and didn't have a clue what to say. So I started off, "Lord, thank you for this food..." Then I started to think, "What else can I say?" I began to tremble and sweat. Finally when I couldn't stand it any longer I said 'amen'.

There are different fractal patterns in the way people pray. Permit me to list a few patterns:

- We end our prayer 'asking in Jesus name', which means asking according to His merit or what we believe He would ask. But sometimes it is used like a formula that must be repeated at the end of the prayer or else it may not work.
- The word 'just' is used a lot, as in 'Lord we *just* ask you...' I don't think this is necessary.
- A very sophisticated pattern is used, as in a pastoral prayer. This may be welcomed from the pulpit but it is not good for saying grace because the food gets cold.
- Sometimes in small groups, prayer requests are shared for 20 minutes and prayer is offered for 5 minutes or less. Shouldn't it be the other way around?

Conversational prayer

A new believer doesn't know any of these patterns and some of them we may not want them to learn. How about we teach young believers that prayer is a conversation? We don't expect young children to say complete sentences but to freely express their thoughts. So let's give young believers permission to learn this way.

I suggest we use the 1-breath 'rule'. Express a thought with one lungful of air. Then stop and let someone else continue. The leader can prime the pump by suggesting they follow the pattern of each change of topic, such as "Lord I thank you for many blessings we have received" (pause). Another person adds "thank you for Jesus" (pause) and another "and for this time together in your Word (pause) etc. When there finally is a break, a new theme is introduced. In the space of 10 minutes you can pray 5 or 6 times even if it is a big group.

This also develops an interesting mutual interdependence since you can't pray what you want all at once. One must stop, listen and think then wait for a pause. Your mind does not wander and the Holy Spirit prompts with ideas and thoughts. I would hazard to say, don't spend much time at all sharing the request before you pray. Just say it as part of the prayer. Others will soon enough know what to pray, each adding a brief petition.

We do not have to worry about micro-managing exactly what we will say. Encourage young believers to pour out their requests without worry how it sounds. The Scriptures say that we don't know how to pray anyway, so the Holy Spirit takes our half formed prayer and reinterprets it before the Father in His own special way.[63]

Reaching out by listening

This can actually lead to reaching out to others in a compassionate way. Supposing the home group decides that we will ask people if they would like prayer for their needs. We have Jesus' example where He asked the blind man "What do you want me to do for you?[64] He could have simply prayed for him without asking. In Deuteronomy 4:7 we are asked "What other nation is so great as to have their gods near them the way the LORD our God is near us whenever we pray to Him?" The answer is none. Our God has a reputation for hearing the prayer of His people especially before the watching nations. So the group decides, we will pray for people's needs and follow Jesus' example by asking people what they would like prayer for.

In our interaction in the world, we keep our ears open for any needs around us that God could possibly meet and we ask for prayer requests. We need to be very clear about what we promise to do and what we can't do. We promise we will fervently pray for the request. We also can help give toward that need if it is appropriate both in service and in resources. We do not promise how God will answer our prayer because we don't know. We do ask the person to keep her eyes open for any sense of how God may be answering that prayer and let us know so we can thank Him. We can say something like:

> "We have a group that likes to pray for people's needs. If it is OK with you, I could share this request with my friends. What do you want Jesus to do for you? We don't know how God will answer but if you could let us know what happens, we would like to thank God for any answers He gives. You would be welcome to thank God with us if you want."

It is important that the focus is on what they would like Jesus to do for them and not on how we are praying. We want faith to be based on Jesus not on our prayer ability (Rees, 1997, p. 68).

Then during the home group meeting we do the following:

1. Ask if anyone has an answer to prayer to report. This really inspires faith as we take time to thank God.
2. Ask if there any new prayer requests which people share very briefly. These are prayed for one by one as they are shared.
3. Both the requests and answers are recorded in a notebook.
4. Earlier prayer requests are prayed for again as time permits.
5. Periodically we could invite others who have received answers to prayer to join us for a time of thanksgiving. This is not meant to ambush them with the Gospel but as we pray, remember together all that Jesus has done. Our guests are welcome to continue with us to learn more. Be sure to make it a comfortable social time and being sensitive to their needs as new comers. (They are not expected to pray out loud but may want to express their thanks by sharing with the group.)
6. This activity need only take 15 or 20 minutes of the home group meeting and can be combined with sharing thoughts from the devotional time and from the Bible study topic.

---

[63] Romans 8:26

[64] Mark 10:51

The practice of listening prayer is great training for this kind of outreach. The Holy Spirit can lead us to pray for something not even mentioned in the request. Once I remember the group praying for someone with a certain sickness and one person prayed for blessing on his sleep which was not part of the request. Later that person reported back to the group "So far nothing has happened concerning my sickness but I am sleeping better than ever before!" Often they are very eager to attribute it as an answer from God.

I have also observed how different spiritual gifts are shown in this kind of ministry. Some people seem to be prayer request magnets. Wherever they go, they have the courage to ask and people warm up to them. Others have the gift of faith when they pray and can boldly approach the Throne of Grace on behalf of these people. Others have the gift of mercy and even as the group prays, they are thinking of things they can do to obtain resources to help meet the needs. It is an exciting team ministry.

Observe the integration of gifts and actions that spring from this prayer:

- Listening to the Holy Spirit in how to pray.
- Listening in how to reach out to others. Taking steps of faith to ask.
- Seeking to meet real needs with God's resources and using our personal resources to help overcoming evil with good.[65]
- Different gifts are in operation in a small group context. People see this and can encourage others to do the same as part of the scale up process.

In spite of our Canadian society being distrustful to discuss spiritual issues, people are quite open to receive prayer. They may be reluctant to discuss their beliefs right off the bat, but they are open spiritually and this prayer experience may be a doorway to an awareness of a deeper need for God.

God does not always answer the prayer the way that is hoped. All we can do is pray. But in His mercy, people are given an opportunity to receive mercy and grace in their time of need. This need not come with manipulation or any kind of pressure. We love people and desire that they too receive the benefits of drawing closer to the throne of Grace.[66] This can lead to wanting to know the God who is on that throne. I would sooner err on reaching out and asking on behalf of others and risking their disappointment than not asking because God might not answer the way we hope. "You have not because you do not ask"[67] gives us cause for serious reflection in why more people are not sharing in the blessing of all the Jesus came to do.

There are many other prayer tools that we could discuss such as anointing the sick, practicing prayer vigils, prayer chains and organizing intercession. I think the supernatural intervention of God needs to be part of the fractal. Someone called this being 'practising super-naturalists' (PSN).We grow as PSN's as we learn to pray under adverse circumstances. I remember being in a bus in Nicaragua on a mission trip when the engine wouldn't start in a rough area of town as it was getting dark. I asked the passengers to get out and stand out by the front of the bus and we were going to pray. We laid hands on the bus and prayed. Before the driver tried to start the engine, we asked that everyone be seated again ready to go. The engine started on the first try. Lessons like this are not quickly forgotten. It was in observing how Jesus faced needs in prayer that the disciples asked him, "Lord, teach us to pray".[68]

---

[65] Romans 12:21
[66] Hebrews 4:16
[67] James 4:2b
[68] Luke 11:1-4

For discussion:

1. What fractal patterns do you observe in prayer personally and in your church?
2. How would you like to see those patterns be changed?
3. What promises in the Bible are important for you concerning prayer?

For personal reflection:

Is there a prayer pattern being reproduced in your church ministry structure that is believer driven and Holy Spirit dependent? Is there a sense that young believers can pray about everything. (Yes it is good to pray about the unemployed and the sick). Are you seeing young believers grow in their ability to become practicing super-naturalists?

Section 4: The Learning Journey

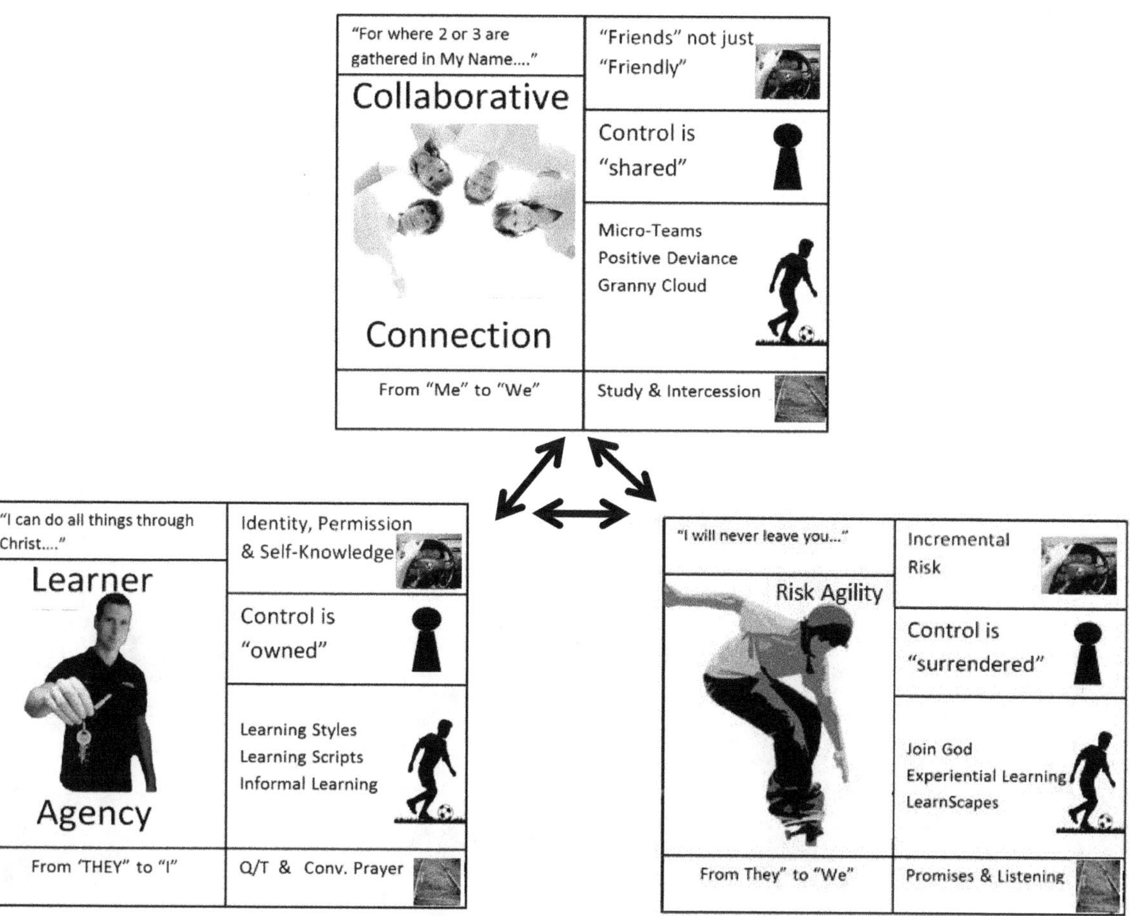

Figure 22: The Learning Journey Model

We often discuss *what* disciples should learn but do not talk much about *how* they should learn. This is important especially if the 'how' we are currently using may not be as effective for some people as other options. Followers of Jesus are *learners* of Him, so this ability to learn, partner with others and cross our comfort zones must be integrated with the actual content of our learning.

In this section we will look at:

- Chapter 9 Learner Agency
- Chapter 10 Collaborative Connection
- Chapter 11 Risk Agility

Chapter 9: Learner Agency

Figure 23: Iris gaining 'walking agency'.

Imagine the hours of coaching it took to get Iris to take some steps: hundreds of hours of holding, lifting, supporting, playing, falling and encouraging. And then at some point, the magical realization by the child, "I can walk!" When that happens, this child has agency, the ability to carry out something. This comes from the Latin *agere* which means *to do.* The word *agile* comes from the same root, so we can think of agency as *a growing ability to do something.* A toddler walks, but with increased agency the young child runs, with all that is implied in choice, balance, speed, skill and especially the ability to go wherever and whenever she/he wants.

Agency in learning

I love to study and learn but it was not always that way. I remember in Kindergarten the shame I felt when the teacher stopped the class to show them the sheet I was working on as an example how *not* to fold the paper and practice printing the letter "F". I did it as well as I could, but somehow I got the blank spaces and F's mixed up and by then it was in a mess I couldn't fix. Everybody stared at it. Then there was the time in Grade Three during the cursive writing test, the teacher asked me why I was looking at the printed alphabet (I was counting the letters to be able to recognize the equivalent on the cursive chart). I didn't even remember taking up writing and there we were in a middle of a test! I won't even talk about the battle I had with long division. All through elementary school I felt as though I was tuned to a different channel and just didn't have good reception.

Then in Grade Six my brother and I were placed in a class that offered extra challenges, more reading, more discussion, more field trips, more exploring and suddenly I felt as if I woke up. I didn't even know I had been 'sleeping' before that, I just thought I was not smart. I don't know how the school recognized that this type of learning would help us, but I am so thankful they did. We were given agency.

We could define *learning agency* as:

> The self-determining capability of shaping one's own life (and therefore one's own learning) based on the individual's sense of self' skills, self-knowledge and available resources. A learner with agency senses permission to develop and use strategies that enable her/his success. A passive or dependent learner exercises no agency but requires constant instruction in every step, takes no initiative, and will not exercise "ownership" of the activity.[69]

Consider the potential for learner agency for the student with the skill and motivation to use a smart phone. These are the new "free agent learners" who can access and network at a touch of a screen. We can call this *un-tethered, self-directed* or *anytime-anywhere learning*. These students want interactivity and personalized learning tools to facilitate collaboration. They are experts at personal data aggregation (a fancy term for finding stuff on the Web). (Covelli, 2010)

How can we develop learner agency? We build a sense of identity and permission to explore, innovate and do. We build risk agility by celebrating all attempts and learning from errors. We equip the learner to take initiative, network with others and 'own' their learning experience.

Educational psychology uses a term, 'locus of control', to describe the degree that individuals choose learning topics and opportunities (an internal locus) or only responds to what others tell them they should learn (external locus). One way to identify an external locus is if we feel it is always someone else's fault why we can't learn[70]. There is a natural progression in the social learning fractal from external to internal control. Think of bike riding, learning to eat or to drive the car. We start with low agency but as proficiency is gained we drive, ride or eat whatever.

---

[69] (Contestable, 2010) (Anderson & McCormic, 2005)

[70] This is not the same as why a course is not passed since that also depends on the fairness of the instructor.

Identity and permission

Imagine what it was like to have the Father speak over Jesus' life saying: "This is My Son, whom I love; with Him I am well pleased." (Matthew 3:17). We all probably need to hear our parents and authority figures speak that over our lives to help us realize all that is at our possibility. This is one of our benefits for being "in Christ".

Attributes of agency for the Jesus learner:

- Learners of Jesus are called children of God. Not only *are* we children of God, but that we are *called* this as well which has an empowering effect. "See what great love the Father has lavished on us, that we should be called children of God! And that is what we are! " (1John3:1a)
- The learner can go anywhere: "Go into all the world...." Matthew 28:19
- The learner can ask anything: "And I will do whatever you ask in My name, so that the Father may be glorified in the Son." John 14:13
- The learner's mentor is always present: "I am with you always (Matthew 28:20) but very truly I tell you, it is for your good that I am going away. Unless I go away, the Advocate will not come to you; but if I go, I will send Him to you." (John 16:7) We think access to the Internet is powerful, what about the presence of God Himself in our lives as the ultimate power supply and source of wisdom!
- The learner can have a "can-do" attitude to every challenge: "I can do all things through Christ who strengthens me." (Phil 4:13)
- The learner has true freedom: "Now a slave has no permanent place in the family, but a son belongs to it forever. [36] So if the Son sets you free, you will be free indeed. (John 8:35,36)

What should the learning look like for this kind of people? Is the Bible exaggerating in offering us such tremendous scope and freedom to learn? Don't we tend to downplay this and limit people to a more passive learner role? (And then blame them for their lack of initiative when they are simply doing what our structures taught them to.) Instead of releasing Jesus learners into adventure, we line them up and take away their agency by teaching them to be completely dependent on being told what to do all the time.

Agency resources and self -knowledge

An agent has resources and is aware of them, knows how to accesses them and is increasingly proficient in their use. Resources include: the knowledge and ability to choose, available time to act and reflect on the actions, practice and feedback on decision with others, discovery and learning from errors, and access to tools and training in their use.

One of the greatest resources is to *know yourself as a learner*. Self-knowledge can inform our choices so that we can be more effective. These include learning styles, learning scripts and how we learn informally.

There are at least 4 types of learning styles: visual, auditory, read/write and kinaesthetic[71]. The sermon, like many lecture formats, really gives an advantage to those who are auditory learners. Those who need to incorporate movement into their learning are disadvantaged in traditional church. As kids they will be asked if they have "ants in their pants" and be told that if they really loved Jesus they would sit still and listen. I am sure in Jesus' time these types of learners would be moving around as they listened. Today you will find these learners standing in the back of the church, coming in and out, doodling or talking during the sermon.

One friend of mine, who has his PhD, is very intelligent but is not an auditory learner. When I found this out, I asked him how he listens to sermons. He said as a kid he liked to pick a colour of someone's clothing and imagine a ball bouncing from person to person with the same colour. The challenge was to see how many bounces he could make before he picked another colour. This coping strategy probably kept him from getting into trouble but didn't help him learn. He once said to me," If you really want me to pay attention to what you are saying, put it in a graph!" He would have been in the front row at the feeding of the 5000, observing how Jesus broke the bread, divided up the baskets and had the crowd seated. He probably would have been the boy who donated his lunch!

We also can have learning scripts. They are like the script of a play that tells us what we should or shouldn't do when it comes to learning about God. The script might be that "only the pastor or minister is really authorized to study the Bible", or that our job is to "sit sown, shut up and listen". The script might be that church is boring as so we see everything about God that way. (I am sure that watching the feeding of the 5,000 wasn't boring!)

Scripts are 'personal learning fractals' that form patterns we repeat whenever we approach learning. It might be negative messages such as "I can't learn a certain subject" or a positive script like "I love learning new things" or "this is fun to practice when I can participate with others".

[71] The VARK test helps you identify which learning style best suits you. http://www.vark-learn.com/english/page.asp?p=questionnaire They also provide strategies to improving your learning ability based on your learning style. (Used with permission)

T.
R.
U.
S.
T.

Figure 24: T.R.U.S.T builds agency

A learning script that supports self-organizing learning[72] is summarized by the acronym TRUST.

- TRUST that the learner is motivated and capable of learning and discovering.
- RELY on the curiosity and interaction of learners to become a catalyst for learner engagement.
- UNCOUPLE your need for the ego boost of being in control.
- Make SPACE for something to happen without turning it into a programmed response.
- Allow enough TIME for learning and discovery to happen versus the express route of forced feeding.

Imagine the release of learning that could happen through TRUST with everyone in the congregation discovering, practicing, experiencing and multiplying this in others. Imagine people choosing what they most need to learn according to their particular circumstances. Imagine people influencing their individual learning networks with what they are discovering. If TRUST was built into our learning DNA, the discipleship learning process could scale up without difficulty.

Informal learning is the fruit of learner agency. Someone likened it to the white space in Figure 25 with the dark space representing formal learning such as sermons and courses. Formal teaching should occupy about 20% of our learning. It should focus on teaching us HOW to learn, how build learner agency and tips to help us reach further in our particular quest. Then 80% of our learning should be untethered, self-directed and applied to where we most need it and are motivated to learn. [73]Can you imagine the release of potential if all of a congregation was empowered with learner agency and week by

Figure 25: Informal Learning is the white space. Source unknown.

[72] Self-organizing learning is when it is learners themselves who initiate and control the learning process.

[73] To see how Math is being taught in order to maximize the role of the formal learning watch: http://www.ted.com/talks/salman_khan_let_s_use_video_to_reinvent_education.html

week discovered, applied, shared and learned! What type of system is needed for that to happen in our communities of faith? One friend commented "How can we help complacent learners? It sounds like it is related to this learner agency you are talking about."

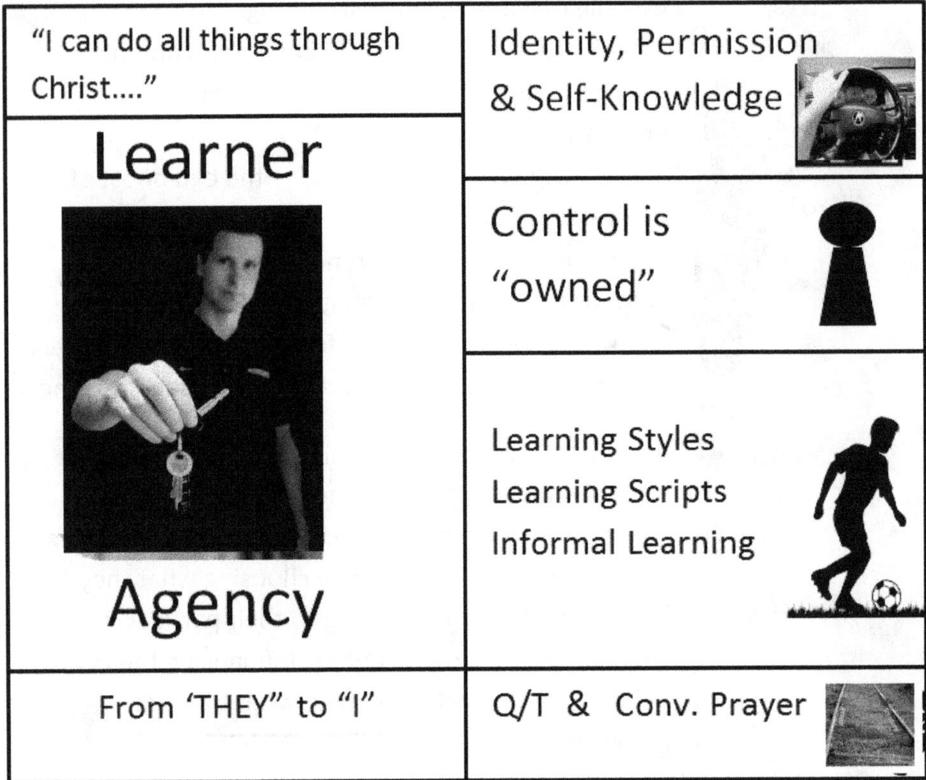

Figure 26: The Learner Agency Model

Note the characteristics summarizing learner agency in Figure 26. The car keys represent self- discovery. The power supply is provided by devotional life in the Scriptures (Quiet Time) and conversational prayer. This conversation of listening and responding to God is an important skill to connect the learner with who they are in Christ, the presence of God within and discovering and learning about ourselves, God, others and creation.

For discussion:

1. Take the Vark Test[63] and reflect on ways you have observed yourself learn. There are suggestions for each learning style on the web site. If the group is big enough, meet with others who have similar styles and compare notes on how you cope with learning.
2. What 'learning scripts" do you have about church? What ways could you make it more "experiential"?
3. The "sandbox" principle is used in teaching people how to use software where they are given an access to a set-up and encouraged to go play and do not worry about "breaking anything". What would a 'sandbox' for discipling others look like?
4. What learning scripts could be improved by applying the TRUST principles to learning? If you were the leader of a congregation, would that make you nervous or would it energize you? What if learning got out of control and people learned what you didn't know? What if you disagreed?
5. Think about what it means to have learner agency in learning about God. Are there things you can't learn because of someone else's action (either, church, pastor or other individuals)? What does that suggest about learner agency?

For personal reflection:

1. Reflect on God speaking over your life: "This is My beloved son/daughter..." How does it make you feel? How does it empower you as a learner?
2. In your faith community what evidence is there that learner agency is valued? To what degree can the programme be allowed to change in order to introduce more experiential opportunities? At what point should experiential learning issues be determined by the learners themselves as they come to the Scriptures?

Chapter 10: Collaborative Connection

Figure 27: Gord and Jim

My friend Gord Jones explains it this way: supposing there is *Gord* and he is working with *Jim* on a project. There is what *Gord* knows and does, and there is what *Jim* knows and does. But there is also *Gord-Jim* (Gord hyphen Jim). This is different than just *Gord* or just *Jim*. This relationship is a hyphenated reality or, as the title of this chapter says, a collaborative connection.

What I have noticed with ideas born from *Gord-Jim*, is that we can't remember who had the idea, or where it came from. It belongs to both. It would not have happened if either of us had been absent.

It would be wonderful if we had churches full of disciples where learner agency is practiced. I think we would be amazed at the results. This is necessary but not sufficient for radical transformation in discipleship. It must also involve some kind of interaction between disciples[74]. I have often thought of

[74] This was discussed in the "we" passages of Chapter7.

growth in learning as mostly an individual's responsibility. I look at it much differently now. "None of us know as much as all of us." We will never accomplish individually what we could accomplish collectively. We need to discover the collaborative connection, the hyphenated reality between believers.

Tool that help build collaborative connection

We would like to discuss three tools that build collaborative connection: micro-teams, positive deviance and the Granny cloud. You may find these terms confusing but we need some new words since we have worn out the old ones. *Fellowship* can mean something quite passive and insipid although not always the case. *Small groups* can be anything. We will use *micro-teams* as the container where collaborative connection is realized[75].

Micro-teams

Let's say we want to get a group of people to get together to do something significant for Jesus. How many people do we need as a minimum? Do we need a few hundred present for God to do something special? Would it work if we had fifty people? Actually it is when two or three gather in His name that He promises to be present.[76] I find that very reassuring for world transformation because there are so many circumstances when it may be difficult to get any more than a few present but we need never be limited by numbers. Two or three could meet anywhere, anytime, for a coffee, for a walk or in a kitchen. And the greatest thing of all is that Jesus promises to be there!

A micro-team can be smaller than a small group. In fact a small group could consist of a number of micro-teams. The teams are not static because all they need to do is to gather once in order to exist. They could re-gather in a different combination tomorrow and the promise of Jesus' presence would still be valid. One could gather once or a hundred times with the same two or three and it would still work. It works if there are more than three people although the more people there are, the more effort it will be taken to organize. Micro-teams are very fluid.

The micro-team is the perfect experiential ministry group. It is a size that is easily formed without any complicated structure. It needs no authorization other than those who are themselves participating. It needs only one person with faith willing to ask one or two to join and wanting Jesus there to teach them something as His disciples.

The micro-team is beautifully illustrated in the friends who brought their paralyzed friend to Jesus:[77]

- Perhaps it started with 1 person caring about his friend who was paralyzed. This person obviously had *agency*.
- He recruiting a few friends to help him.
- They didn't have much of a plan other than getting their friend to Jesus.

---

[75] 1 Corinthians 12 is an excellent illustration of Micro-teams in action

[76] Matthew 18:20

[77] Mark 2:3-12; Luke 5:17-26

- They solved problems along the way such as how to get past the crowds to see Jesus and how to get a few needed supplies like a rope and carrier of some sort.
- They risked doing something never recorded before or after in the Scriptures: they dug a hole in the roof and lowered their friend into Jesus' presence.
- It would have been a very messy job, and possibly dangerous. The people below would have been choked with dust and very uncomfortable. Their friend could have fallen and the roof could have collapsed. People surely complained and possibly had been very angry. That is except for Jesus who wasn't angry. He saw their faith and healed the man.

I love this story because it is so unsanitized. It really showed the love this micro-team had for their friend and how they put their faith into action. They didn't have to wait for the programme. Or wait until a hundred people agreed to make a hole in the roof, or have a vote. All they had were a few friends ready to do something in Jesus' name together.

A micro-team is flexible, focused and agile.

A micro-team is flexible in *meeting size* because it will work for any number of two or more. It is flexible in *meeting frequency* because it can meet only once or regularly. It is flexible in *meeting length* because it can do something together for 5 minutes or 5 months. It is flexible in *meeting location* because it can happen anywhere, at any time, over the phone, on the Internet or face-to-face.

A micro-team is focused. It is *focused in objective* because it is gathering in Jesus' name to do something. It is *focused in faith* because of the conviction that Jesus' presence is absolutely necessary for an acceptable outcome.

A micro-team is agile because it needs *no external organizing* and no *additional authorization.* It is free to *experiment in learning* and free to *make mistakes.* It is free to meet *when* it wants and *where* it wants. It can stop meeting and reform itself in an infinite number of ways. A micro-team has agency.

A micro-team is a fractal that can be scaled up as long as members understand that it is their job to take initiative in Jesus' name to gather together to learn and serve.

What will distort the fractal is if people fail to understand it is their responsibility to figure out how to self-organize. If they have to wait for someone else to do it, they will fail. It won't scale up because at some point it will be too complicated to organize. It will also fail if the objectives are externally applied because there is a good chance that it will miss God's purpose at hand. The four friends could have been directed to go listen to Jesus tomorrow when what they really wanted was to bring their paralyzed friend to be healed today. We can't expect a system to be correctly interpreting all that God wants His disciples to be doing in micro-teams throughout the week. We all need to be listening to His guidance, teaming up in a minimum of two or three and stepping out in faith. We all need to be exercising agency.

A micro-team is different than anything in the church because they only need to be shown how and released but not organized. Let them do that to discover, learn and report back. We will be surprised at the amazing diversity and the solutions that will emerge.

Figure 28: Try Stuff is an example of a micro-team event.

Gord and I, in one of our collaborative connections, suggested we call this micro-team process: "Try Stuff". It has very little structure but lots of relational glue. It gives permission to experiment, to see what happens, to take risks and to be safe with each other. I love it. Our leadership projects have been varied, some advancing quickly, others pausing but it is exciting to look back and see a path of new discovery and a broad place to learn. In the short run, it may look like not much is happening. In the long run, powerful lessons are learned.

One important aspect has been the frequency of meeting: about every 5 weeks, giving time to actually try stuff, reflect on it, share what you are discovering and soak up encouragement to take the next step. I am finding it very rewarding not following a formula, but where I can explore the fascination of risk-taking within the safety of a supportive community. It allows for the recurring and sustainable steps to explore, reflect, and act.

Another important application of the TRY Stuff idea as a micro-team is that it does not require massive participation. I am not sure how many church members want to think this way and take the experiential learning risks. But we are not limited by the lack of enrolment. It takes only two or three and others can join in and experience the adventure.

Positive deviance (PD) is a second tool that helps build collaborative connection. This is the principle that people are more likely to *act their way into a new way of thinking* than to t*hink their way into a new way of acting*. Instead of normally front loading information and hoping that will result in a change of behaviour, new behaviour is practiced so that attitudes and internal knowledge can be changed (Sternin, 2007). The biggest challenge is for leaders to relinquish their power to enable others to find their own solutions. The story of PD has been very encouraging in in international development and business where people are equipped to find local solutions and to practice these with others.

You may have heard about positive deviance in Psychology 101. "They call it the "*as if*" phenomenon. If people act "as if" they are who they want to be, very soon they'll naturally be this way because they have changed their thinking. "*Do it afraid*" very soon becomes fearlessness, for example. Positive reinforcement occurs, and the fears are found to be less than once thought, a barrier that can be breached. Thinking proceeds behaviour change, but to change thinking, often the behaviour has to be changed." (McNabb, 2011)

The Granny Cloud is a more passive educational principle but just as important where it was discovered that simply being interested and cheering on others, as grandmothers do for their grandchildren, learning can be considerably enhanced. Often people shy away from mentoring because "they don't know enough". It may not depend on what you know as much as how much you care, in order to help others discover incredible things.

There is a Scriptural Granny cloud mentioned in Hebrews 12:1: "Therefore since we have so great a cloud of witnesses surrounding us..." The knowledge of the saints that have gone before us and are cheering in heaven's grandstand should motivate us to "lay aside every encumbrance and the sin that entangles us" and run the race with endurance, fixing our eyes on Jesus. Like those witnesses, we can also cheer others on here as well. . We don't have to be experts; we simply have to take an interest. [78]

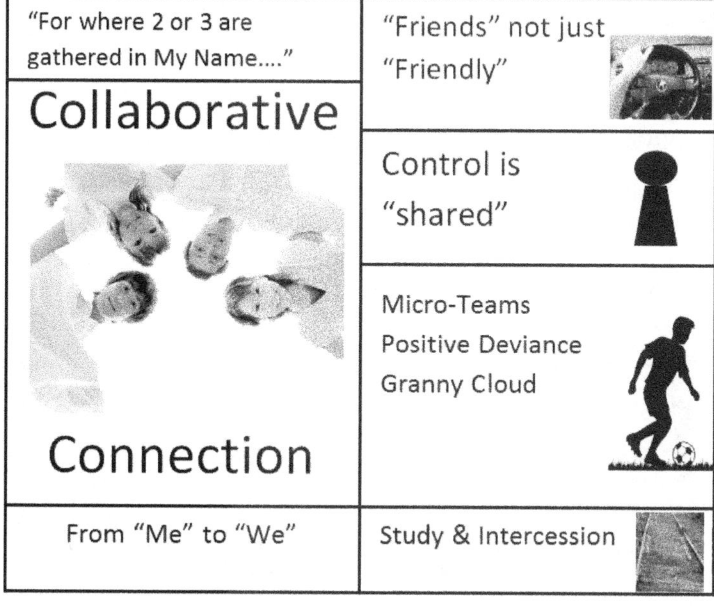

Figure 29: Collaborative Connection

The linked hands (Figure 23) represent the discoveries that emerge from learning to work together and affect the following:

- The focus moves to the plural, "From "me" to "we".
- Control is shared.
- Rather than just 'being friendly' seek to become 'true friends'. Imagine the difference. By very nature this means that one cannot do it massively, but must reproduce through the fractal.
- Scripture/Prayer elements, which empower the process, are increasing in complexity and involve learning to intercede and study the Scriptures.
- Jesus promises that His presence be shown in a special way as soon as we "go plural", that is two or three gathering in His name.

For discussion:

1) Consider the micro-team in the Daniel 3: 8-30 and the appearance of one "like the son of the gods" (v.25). Can you think of other examples of micro-teams in the Scriptures?
2) How do you keep micro-teams self-organizing and flexible? How can too much organizing harm the process?
3) How can this be useful in discipleship? How can it scale up?

[78] See explanation of the Granny cloud in Suguta Mitra's talk http://www.ted.com/talks/lang/eng/sugata_mitra_the_child_driven_education.html

4) What would be the potential influence of millions of micro-teams 'overcoming evil with good' (Romans 12:21)?

For personal reflection:

1) Who has been a micro-team for you on different occasions? If you could TRY STUFF, what would you like to do? Who could you ask to join you?
2) Draw out a diagram of the micro-teams you are involved in. Consider family, friends, faith community, work, interests and volunteer work. What is your contribution in each of the teams? What do you receive from each team? How could these teams be more effective in what they accomplish?
3) Can they stop or change as necessary? Are the members taking personal initiative to try new things and to learn? What would help you make a more significant contribution? What are these teams accomplishing or could accomplish that you can't do by yourself?
4) The best way to understand the meaning of the "with Him" fractal is to think about the differences between "being friendly" and "being a friend" What is it? While there may be some cultural difference in what being a friend means, it is never just superficial, it will always require time and an investment of life shared. Social learning does not mean 'superficial learning'. We must 'be with' those we are discipling. They can tell if we are just being friendly or if we are true friends.

Chapter 11: Risk Agility

Figure 30: On the edge of the pool.

When we first moved to a small town in Nova Scotia and were looking for a place to rent, I remember Naomi saying as we looked at a lovely old apartment house right beside campus, "I think God wants us to live there." I wondered how in the world she thought that. The house had just been sold (but no rental sign was visible). Through the realtor we contacted the new owner who agreed to put us on the waiting list but there were 6 people before us. We prayed and waited and about a month later we phoned again and the owner said, 'Oh didn't I tell you, the apartment is yours." Not only was it a beautiful apartment but I was offered the job as building superintendent so we paid only $150/month rent for the 5 years we lived there. God honoured Naomi's faith as she stepped out in taking a risk

Risk is *faith applied to real world situations*. Nothing happens without it. Learners will not have agency unless they are prepared to risk. Learners cannot connect unless they risk reaching out. And we will not grow as Jesus learners if we do not risk.

Risk means moving from theory to practice. It involves some instruction to point us in the right direction, but relies on observation (seeing something done), experience (trying to do it yourself), reflection (considering how the experience turned out and what could be done to improve it), and repeating the process.

We can design learning processes to be 'theoretical' or 'experiential'. With the former, we can give lectures and test for knowledge, the information is downloaded, memorized and regurgitated. The testing instrument best measures information retrieval. History was taught to me this way and I hated it.

But the same subject can be taught in an experiential way. Instead of being told about World War 2, the class could go visit the Legion, interview some veterans, go to the war museum, and construct maps and battle plans. For young boys who have trouble sitting still, experiential learning could ignite a fascination with history.

Risk means surrendering control because we cannot be absolutely sure what is going to happen. This is why many lessons are taught theoretically and not experientially because the teacher or institution loses some degree of control and cannot guarantee outcomes. (Unless the outcome is to respond to the spontaneous and learn no matter what.)

Jesus used experiential learning all the time with his disciples. He helped them take risks:

- He sent them out two by two to preach, heal and deliver.[79]
- They handled the crowds: "Master, do you want us to send them away?"[80] Then the disciples handed out the food and picked up the leftovers.
- When the disciples pointed out that the crowds were hungry He said "You feed them".[81]
- He let them go through life and death situations and responded to their reactions. "Master don't you care that we are perishing" they cried. "Oh you of little faith" he replied.[82] He even chided them giving them the Great Commission for their unbelief and hardness of heart.[83]
- He took Peter, James and John to the Mount of Transfiguration.[84] Talk about a risk encounter of experiential learning! We can see how they were accustomed to DOING something as a response to Jesus because they offered to build Moses and Elijah a tent.[85]
- They were trying to cast out a demon while Jesus was away and they couldn't so Jesus used it as a teaching opportunity.[86]
- He let them observe His prayer life so they would ask "Lord, teach us to pray".[87]
- He did astounding things like walking on the water and made it into a learning opportunity.[88]
- He asked them to join with Him in prayer at the hour of His testing.[89]
- They observed Jesus interacting with the Pharisees and asked questions "Master You did know that You got the Pharisees really upset with what You said, right?[90]

---

[79] Mark 6:7-13
[80] Mark 6:36
[81] Mark 6:37
[82] Matthew 8:23-27
[83] Mark 16:14
[84] Mark 9:2-13
[85] Mark 9:5
[86] Mark 9:18
[87] Luke 11:1
[88] Matthew 14:24-33
[89] Mark 14:38

- Risks were incremental starting with easier ones and ending with extremely demanding ones (and martyrdom for many).

I have been challenged by Hebrews 6:1 where we are commanded to leave the elementary teachings and go on to maturity. First not all items in the list seems to be that elementary and secondly I had thought that really complicated theology was what followed the elementary teaching. But this is not the case! The verse before[91] talks of experiential learning: “Solid food is for the mature who *because of practice* have their senses trained to discern good and evil” (emphasis added). You don’t get the feeling that solid food is referring to an endless discussion of lofty theology that is removed from a clear expectation of putting the ‘solid food’ into practice. The training of the senses to discern is not a theoretical experience but a hard won conviction in the battlefield. We learn by doing and once we get the basics, the solid food is concrete acts of “one another” ministry, using gifts, serving the disadvantaged and overcoming evil with good.[92]

There is also a rhythm for experiential learning. If you don’t get this right, it can be extremely uncomfortable and even counterproductive. Consider teaching a child how to swing. Imagine you are pushing the swing while calling out how to ‘pump’ your feet. You push, take a step back, wait and just as the swing is as far back as it will go, you push again (position C) If you get the timing and positioning right it takes only a very little push. If you get it wrong, (position A or B) you will be hit by the swing,

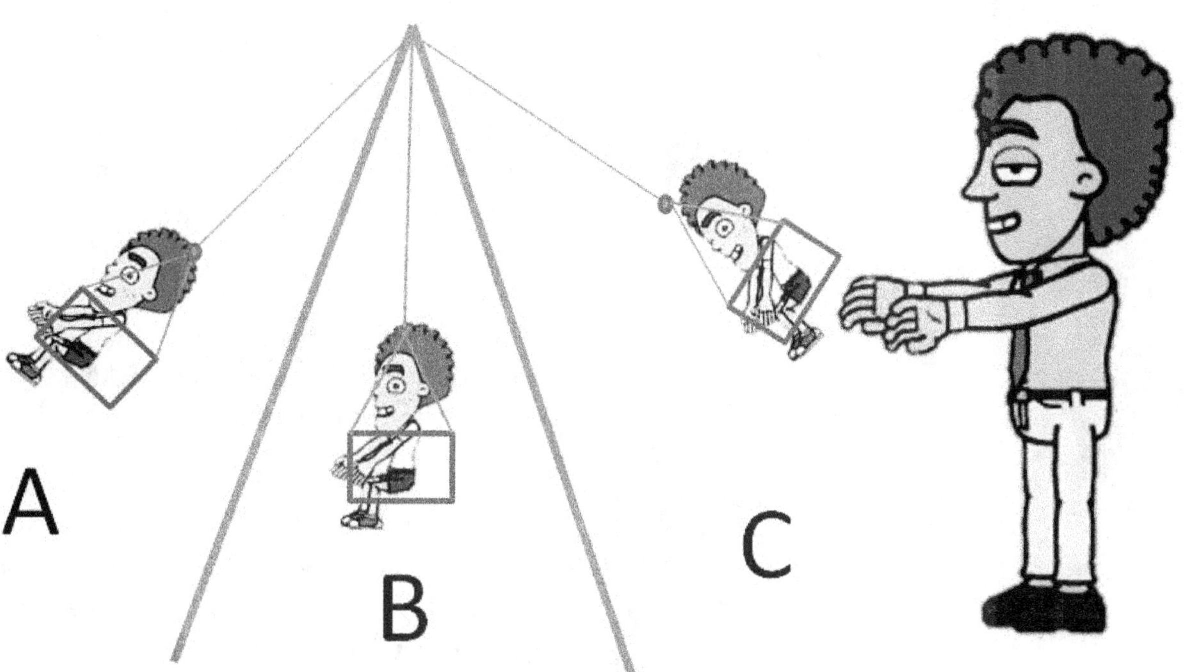

Figure 31: Swing Resonance

[90] Matthew 15:12
[91] Hebrews 5:14
[92] Romans 12

injure the child and very likely discourage the child from wanting to try it again.

Getting on the wave length of the swing motion (which is called resonance) may seem easy but it takes practice. Jesus was a master at this by showing, instructing (not too much), inviting and releasing the disciples, then reflecting together afterward and encouraging them to try again. Mostly it was facilitated by His continual presence with the disciples so He could be there for debriefing and further instruction.

I think we often get the resonance wrong on our initial attempts at experiential learning: the right activities but the wrong timing. People get impatient, confused, cannot process feelings of failure or are overwhelmed by something they didn't expect. The teacher must be aware of all that is going on as well as trying to facilitate the dynamics of the experience. This is often an overload for the teacher who is struggling to multitask and can only be improved by practice. The experience teacher knows how not to interrupt the learners with more instruction until they process the first instruction . It is like allowing them time to exhale and not insisting they take a breath continually[93].

Risk involves finding what God is doing and join Him. Peter practiced this in seeing the Lord walking on the water . He intended to "pass them by" (Mark 6:48). What a provokation for learning! It caused Peter to call out and be commanded to join him (Matthew 14:30). He did pretty well until he saw the wind (v.30). Jesus rescued him then rebuked the storm.

Henry Blackaby has some interesting ideas on risk. He says "Christians ought not to be smothered in fear". And asks "if God will ever ask you to do something you are not able to do? The answer is yes--all the time! It must be that way, for God's glory and kingdom. If we function according to our ability alone, we get the glory; if we function according to the power of the Spirit within us, God gets the glory. He wants to reveal Himself to a watching world." He suggests, that "when you see God at work around you, your heart will leap inside you and say, "Thank you, Father for letting me be involved where you are." When I am surrounded by God's activity and God opens my eyes to recognize His work, I always assume He wants me to join Him. (Blackaby, Blackaby, & King, 2008, p. 113 and other sources)

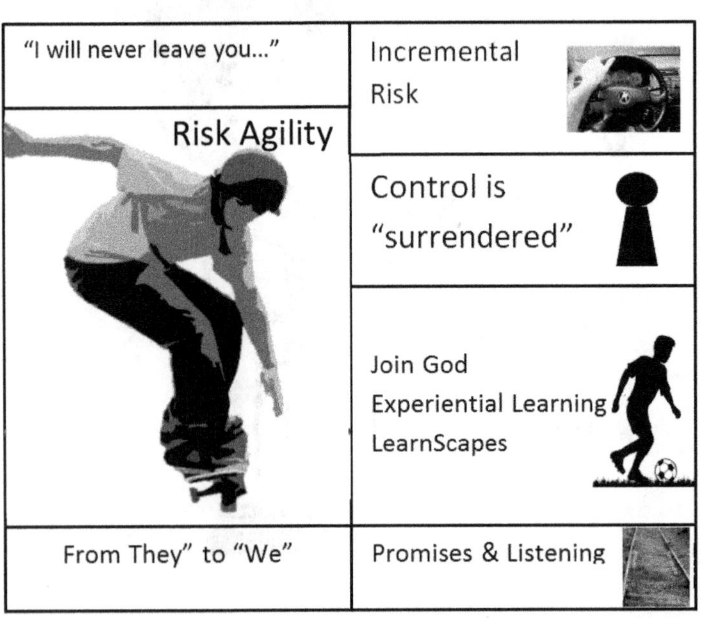

Figure 32: Risk Agility

This challenges me as I read it because I think I spend a lot of energy trying to eliminate risk instead of finding out what God wants us to do in that situation and calculating the risk that should be invested in it. (Luke 14:28). One author calls it

[93] Personal communication with John Klaas

"building the bridge as you walk on it".[94]

The skateboard is perhaps a good image for risk agility although it would be better if there were more people involved. Control is surrendered at this stage since risk means that outcomes are often beyond our control. As we risk in reaching out to more people they move dfrom being "they" to becoming "we" as relationships are connected and agency is shared.

The power track of the Word and prayer should emphasize the Promises in the Scriptures and listening prayer to tune outselves to what God is doing so we can join Him.

For discussion:

1. Look at the number of times Jesus addressed His disciples as "You ... of little faith" (Matthew 6:30, 8:26, 14:31 16:8). Was this His nickname for the disciples or did they need continual correcting? How do you feel about this as an experiential learning strategy?

For personal reflection:

How willing are you to step out of comfort limits and safety to risk creatively serving God? Who is joining you in that? Think of a big risk. Is there any way you can break that down into smaller steps.

---

[94] "'*Building the Bridge As You Walk On It'* tells the personal stories of people who have embraced deep change. It inspired author Robert Quinn to take his concept one step further and develop a new model of leadership—'the fundamental state of leadership'. The exploration of this transformative state is at the very heart of the book. Quinn shows how anyone can enter the fundamental state of leadership by engaging in the eight practices that center on the theme of ever-increasing integrity--reflective action, authentic engagement, appreciative inquiry, grounded vision, adaptive confidence, detached interdependence, responsible freedom, and tough love. After each chapter, Quinn challenges you to assess yourself with respect to each practice and to formulate a strategy for personal growth." http://www.leadershipnow.com/leadershop/7112-X.html

Section 5: Assembling the Fractal

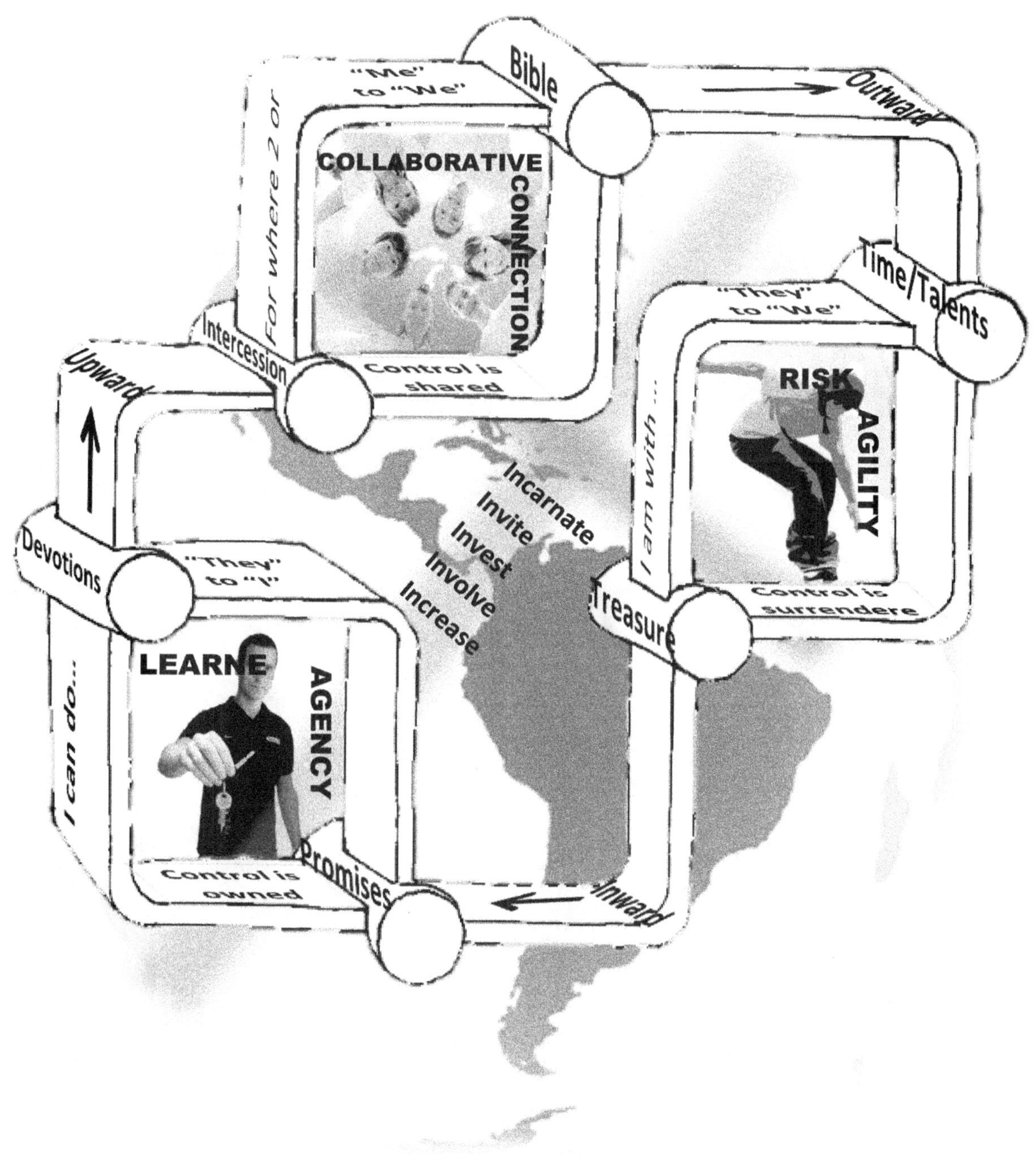

Figure 33: The Discipleship Fractal

We need to assemble the fractal, which contains biblical patterns, adult learning principles, proper communication and a narrative that captures the imagination in order to mobilize learners. This is a complex process of discovery and experimentation. Jesus is our model, method and message in the discipleship process. We will experiment as to how this could be assembled and will include:

Chapter 12: The Story

Figure 34: Dan Officer demonstrating how he gets into bed.

There is a story behind this photo from our family's visit to Argentina a few years ago. At the time, I didn't want to inquire too deeply into what was going on but this is what I pieced together. We would hear someone running down the hallway of the hotel and then a bump. This would be followed by absolute gales of laughter. Later I found this action shot in the camera featuring Dan Officer, our son-in-law. I know that our sons Dan and Tim also enjoyed their part in this photographic learning project.[95] But then again they came from a long line of story tellers so I am not surprised.

Oh I loved it when the kids were little and we were sitting around the campfire and they would ask for another "Ernest Slaberhawk" story[96]. These were always about some mishap I had when I was growing up and no matter how often they heard them, they loved to hear about "The exploding diaper"[97] or "The frying pan and the forest fire"[98]

The power of story

We want to look at the power of story and how it captures meaning with very few words; inspires our imagination; awakens passion; explains why we are doing what we are doing; tells us what to do next; answers peoples' questions; helps us find ourselves and passes easily from person to person.

---

[95] This was first told in The 1 Minute Learner: http://www.devedinternational.net/1ml/1ml-031/player.html .

[96] A fictitious name invented by Alexis, our daughter.

[97] The first time I tried wringing out a disposable diaper and it exploded all over the bathroom of the house we were visiting.

[98] The Boy Scout camp where I helped battle a forest fire with a cast iron frying pan.

Jesus was a master story teller. "The kingdom of God is like …." and off He would go. "Beware of the leaven of the Pharisees…" and everyone would lean forward to try to catch every word. The crowds loved it even if the Pharisees got upset.

One of His stories was great for the bunch of fishermen He was recruiting. "Follow Me and I will make you fishers of men!" (Matthew 4:19). It so captured their imagination that they left their nets to follow Jesus. I have to admit I don't find this fishing story very motivational. Anytime I tried getting the hook out of the fish's mouth, it always seemed damaging to the fish and not an apt image of helping others be blessed by God. But to professional fishermen who used nets, this story was exactly the story that would speak to them of purpose and meaning.

The right story easily captures the meaning with very few words. I am sure you heard the joke of the new prisoner who was listening to the old inmates tell jokes. "37!" one would say and they all would laugh. Or "42!" and they would all laugh again. The young prisoner asked what it meant and he was told that these jokes had been told so many times that they decided to give them numbers to make it easier. So the young man said "27!" but nobody laughed. When he asked why they remained silent, he was told, "The problem is that some people just can't tell a good joke."

Figure 35: A drawing by Alexis Officer

The right story inspires our imagination and awakens passion. Look how this charcoal sketch (Fig. 35) with its simplicity of lines creates the feeling of peace and tranquility of a misty morning. It makes me want to go get my binoculars and go birding. I can imagine myself on the trail and enjoying the blessing of watch this pair of grebes swim by.

The right story explains to us why we are doing what we are doing. Jesus said we are to be salt with flavour, a light on a stand. Not hidden but shared. *Not* flavourless but influencing everything like yeast in the dough or salt in the soup.

The right story tells us what to do next (and what not to do). Some good friends, Gord and Margaret Jones, decided to build a library to house their collection of 45,000 books. They decided to use the idea of a barn on the farm where Gord grew up. The barn was rustic and not easily damaged, had open spaces and lots of flexibility in how it could be used. This worked for their library idea. When the Jones' didn't know what to do, they would ask "What would make it more like a barn?" The story guided their decisions.

The right story answers peoples' questions. Think of the story, "why people go to church?" How would non-church-attenders answer that? Imagine if we could give them a story that would help them understand the blessing of being together in community, the joy of worship and the peace from prayer together. What story would invite them in? What story would help us reach out to them?

The right story helps us find ourselves. In the parable of the talents we could be the person with many talents or the person with only one so in all ways we can relate to what Jesus said. We can identify with finding a treasure, or witnessing a house destroyed by a flood or understanding how faith is like a tiny seed. We need to be able to relate to it easily. Jesus told His stories in an agrarian economy. He would not necessarily use the same images to help people relate to the ideas today.

The right story will be told and retold far more often than we could ever imagine. You may have seen the YouTube video of the Flash mob singing the Hallelujah Chorus in the shopping centre. It 'went viral' where it got passed around faster than the common cold. In the space of two months almost thirty million viewers watched it[99]. A typical choir never has that type of exposure. Surprise, humour, the contrasting setting, the wonder of the people and the beauty of the music, all contributed to a stunning performance, and captured our attention so that we wanted others to see.

If the story fits the culture it becomes a sticky message. Like the hook on burdock seeds, the message stays with us.[100] The book *Made to Stick* (Chip Heath, 2007) states the message needs to be simple, unexpected, concrete, credible, emotional and stories-based for it to stick. [101]

The story element is often missed in documents where we declare our purpose such as mission and vision statements. We need them to be clear, concise and sticky.

What story best explains discipleship? Supposing we get all the elements right in the fractal design, how are we going to capture the imagination of the church? How will people get interested? What will they tell others? To call it a church programme just won't work. Add it to the usual thirty minutes of church announcements and it will be neglected. It will be about as attractive as eating supper by yourself in front of the TV.

The story will need to capture real meaning of relationships: nothing cheap and shallow, nothing manipulative and glitzy. We will have to be able to imagine ourselves in the story with the time and ability to respond. It must have a sense of freedom to adjust to varying demands. It will need something of the comfort of our home while offering a challenge to make a difference in the world. It will need to be something everybody can do, that they can 'own' and develop, so it does not load church staff with impossible demands of administration.

---

[99] Hallelujah Flash Mob: http://www.youtube.com/watch?v=SXh7JR9oKVE

[100] The Sticky Message http://www.devedinternational.net/1ml/1ml-051/player.html

[101] This is a great tool to evaluate the stickiness of our discipleship message. The authors give lots of examples of evaluation.

The story of the *Four Rooms.*

Imagine a house that had four rooms: a café, a workshop, a patio and a market. You can use any of the rooms whenever you want and whenever there is a need. There is a family life celebrated in the rooms whenever gathering happens. It feels like 'home'.

The Café is the place where two people meet to talk about their journey, just like friends meeting for coffee. This is the space where some of the tools of discipleship can be practiced and so that the person receiving the discipling has an example to follow in helping someone else.

The Workshop is where you can get sawdust on the floor and your hands dirty. It is a place of experimenting with ideas, making things and preparing to serve God and others.

The Patio is a place for relaxing after a day's work. I noticed on mission trips where members liked to gather, reflect and share about their day, usually offering amazing times of prayer and sharing.

Finally the Market is the place of interaction in the world where people can "buy without money and without cost".[102] It is our interface with neighbours, coworkers and friends where people become attracted to the story all about Jesus.

Figure 36: The Four Rooms

What I like about the four rooms idea is that there is freedom to use the rooms as you find them helpful. Just like at home, we don't have lots of rules about when you can sit in the living room: these rooms are spaces to be used and cared for, just like home.

The story needs to 'feel right' like a pair of old slippers yet at the same time calling out of us to reach for the impossible. That is not easy to find.[103] As you develop the discipleship fractal, test the story for the stickiness and what the story is supposed to accomplish. The story may need adjusting as it relates to difference generations so there should be some capacity for the story to evolve or have different facets to respond to the varying needs.

The some stories we have used to explain church have been very persistent and have promoted passivity and information gathering rather than discipleship. Individuals 'go to' a building rather than 'belong to a people'. They think that by sitting and listening to someone teach that the purpose of church is accomplished, instead of learning together in a life-long journey. People need to see the possibility of 'being with' someone in a discipleship relationship and pass on the experiential learning to

[102] Isaiah 55:1
[103] I wonder if for the next generation the story will be organized around leaving a legacy of philanthropy (Virant, 2011)

the next generation. They need to understand the unchanging nature of the Jesus' Kernel and have the promises of God's power and enabling undergirding all that they do. The four rooms serve as a start but it is too focussed on real estate. We need to find more compelling stories to unstick lesser stories. This may be the greatest challenge of the discipleship fractal.

For discussion:

1. Can you think of stories that have stuck with you from your family?
2. What stories of Jesus are especially meaningful to you? How would He retell them in today's context?
3. What are stories you like to tell about your experience with God and church?
4. What would be a captivating story about discipleship that would fit your community of faith? How does it measure against the sticky message test?
5. For those who like research I have put a project online for this chapter. I have selected a number of websites to practice identify the nucleus, the story, and the essential components of the fractal design. Evaluate for integration of programme and 'stickiness' of message. Use the forum at www.networkchurch.ca to exchange ideas and suggest church/ministry websites that interest you and that illustrate some aspect of a fractal design.

For personal reflection:

What is the story of your life? What will people remember you after you are gone? What is the story you would like them to remember?

Chapter 13: Communication Tools

Figure 37: Paintings by Beth Fellows[104]

Compassion = feel + with

These are 12 paintings by artist Beth Fellows and are all on themes in International development such HIV Aids, empowerment of women, water, environmental disasters etc. Beth combined these paintings with 12 poems written by a colleague of hers. When I saw this collection I wondered what would happen if we combined this with 12 songs by Steve Bell and Stephen Lewis' book *Race against Time* on the Millennium Development Goals. This artistic input was included with 12 Bible passages that spoke on themes of humanity and it was all put into a course called Art in International Development.[105]

The mixture of the various forms of art was particularly effective. I was less experienced with looking at paintings and I remember being impacted how some artists began sharing ideas about colour and composition and it gave me new insight into the issues. I was also deeply moved by viewing the art while listening to music. The combination produced some results that probably neither the painter nor the composer intended.

Why does art work in opening us up to human needs, when just plain information doesn't? We are saturated with information for one thing. We are bombarded with news of disasters unfolding, almost before it happens. So just assuming that more information will motivate for transformation is difficult. We learn to filter it out.

We need to feel passion (to feel intensely or suffer) before we can respond with compassion (to feel intensely with or suffer with). We need to *care about* before we can *care for*. Art can elevate our passion

---

[104] Beth Fellows – Images of Humanity Project. Used with permission.

[105] Inquiries for the Art in International Development course can be sent to jimk@devedinternational.net

about the issue that then can be activated to become compassion for the people affected in ways that pure information cannot do.

"The best art makes your head spin with questions." (Maeda, 2006) We have far too much information with far too little reflection on the underlying questions. Art can provoke these deeper questions that can lead us to change.

The beauty of art offers immense scalability. A song can be effective if listened to by a few or by many. A painting delivers a message no matter how many times it is viewed and over how many years. An effective commercial grabs our attention, stays in our mind and we talk about it with our friends.

We need to ask whether we are communicating with art or with information. Are we just delivering facts or are we helping people to 'feel with' the issue?

Evaluating our message

I am not an advertising expert but there are some basic filters we can use to evaluate our communication:

- Likeability
- Comprehension
- Appropriateness
- Persuasiveness

Likeability includes aspects of empathy, familiarity, entertainment, alienation, confusion and relevance. A well-liked idea will cause a lot of attention evidenced by the Super Bowl ads. If people don't like or don't notice the idea, it is not going anywhere. Think how quickly you turn off certain commercials. Perhaps because I don't watch too much TV, there are some commercials that I enjoy.

Comprehension is whether the message is understood and we can relate to conclusions formed because of imagery and whether we 'get' the story. If people don't understand the message, we fail in our communication with them. Included in this dimension are clarity of expectations and avoiding confusion and not loading on hidden expectations after they 'sign-up'.

Appropriateness measures the comfort level of the message. If I am uncomfortable with the language or images used, I will not engage. This would happen to me for instance if I invited a guest to church and the sermon dealt with how our friends are like fish to be caught. I would be squirming in my seat and my friend would probably not want to visit again. Related to this, is the message communicated in an age-appropriate way? How will people from other cultures react? I have to be able to find myself in the story for it to be appropriate. I need to feel that the story is mine in some way.

Finally our communication should be persuasive. Are people motivated to change as a result of our communication? Are there appropriate venues to respond? Can people freely choose to participate or not? Persuasion is different than coercion. It does not need to be hard sell. For change to be sustainable, I need to believe what is asked of me is possible and that it is something I want. I need to be able to imagine myself experiencing this change.

People telling their story as part of The Story is a powerful communication tool that can bridge all of these dimensions. Especially if the story is brief and simple, people will enjoy paying attention. So coaching may be necessary to help be concise and focus the story telling. As Blais Pascal said, "I would not have made this so long except that I do not have the leisure to make it shorter." (Google)

Fractal resonance

All our communication decisions need to resonate with the fractal. Supposing your fractal is designed to allow for self-organizing learning where participants are encouraged and expected to take initiative in building outreach and discipleship relationships. Yet the communication is highly centralized giving the impression that the leadership is responsible to organize the discipleship programme and that there really is no role for individual initiative. Let me illustrate with a practical example.

Supposing you want men to reach out to other men, meet spontaneously, support each other and take initiative to deepen friendships. There is a men's breakfast organized and it is 'pumped' from the announcements. Men are repeatedly reminded to come. It would be easy for someone to think, "why should I invite someone because anyone who would want to go has already have been invited ten times?"

What would happen if there were no announcements but rather it was decided that the men were in charge of inviting their own guests? Perhaps 4 men were interested and they go out for breakfast. They decided they each invite one person next time, and that this would be the fractal they would follow. Each time one person invites another. First time attendance breakfast would be 4 then 8, then 16 then 32. While this may have slower results at first consider how men receiving a personal invitation would allow for much more effective networking. By wanting to grow too quickly, there is the risk that it would always be the job of leadership to get people there by endless reminders and effectively disempowering the multiplication fractal by individuals caring for and reaching out to others.

For discussion:

1. Do your communication tools allow for the possibilities of scaling-up?
2. Think of commercials that grab your attention and others that make you sleep or feel annoyed. What are the differences?
3. What are some examples of art that clearly produced a particular feeling? (a song, a book, a painting etc.). How could art be used more effectively in your disciple-making fractal?
4. Think of examples where the communication strategy resonates with the fractal or it doesn't.

For personal reflection:

What are your strengths and weaknesses in communication? Who can you work with to build a stronger communication team?

Chapter 14: Putting It All Together

Figure 38: The author winning an encyclopaedia set at 12 years old. —Citizen-UPI staff phot

My five cents worth

I have not won many things in my life but I did win a complete multi-volume World Book encyclopaedia set when I was in Grade Eight by asking a question in a newspaper contest. I borrowed a five cent stamp from my mother with the agreement that if I won, I would pay her back (which I did). So my mother's five cent venture capital investment provided hundreds of hours of enjoyable browsing.

As you can see from the photo, by Grade Eight I was already well on the way to the 'geekiness' that has characterized my life. This gifting, as I would choose to call it, is reflected in this book. I have thought a great deal about these issues and have struggled over them. I am not sure I am correct but rightly or wrongly, I have tried to live the type of discipleship described here. This book is a testament to my five cents worth.

We need to put these fractal ideas into some kind of conclusion. What fractals are just waiting to be discovered that will energize disciple-making in the church today? If you have not yet found such a fractal, it doesn't mean it is not out there. Perhaps small changes could help us gain important perspectives. Consider the subtle but importance of the implications of this question: "What if discipleship was more like a garden than a formula?" (Mowry, 2009, p. 6) This suggests freedom to experiment, permitting variety and preferences, the value of experience, fun, hard work and the joy of harvest. It suggests seasons and the opportunity for a fresh start each year. Contrast this with, a formula suggesting standards, expectations, fault for not following it exactly, and promising guarantees when life does not often work out the way we would like.

There are potentially conflictive patterns in the fractals we are using. Has the clergy/laity divide caused members to think that somehow they are not qualified to make disciples or that it is precisely what they are paying the minister to do? What is the pastor doing in "coming along side others" that members learn by imitation in how to do the same with others? Are the expectations associated with the traditional professional/volunteer division of roles inhibiting members from reproducing a multiplying pattern of disciples which will not scale-up? The repeating patterns we choose have enormous consequences.

What a discipleship fractal must do:

The discipleship system grows by fractal design so we must pay attention to observe and decide whether what is reproduced is what we want. If not, we need to change the pattern (chapters 1, 2). Let's summarize exactly what a discipleship fractal must do or have:

1. THE KERNEL: It is built around an unchanging kernel centred upon the Trinity and God's salvation purpose in Christ. The kernel is about God: first last and always. It is demonstrated both in Jesus' coming and His "with Him" pattern of making disciples. The fractal assumes the active involvement of the Holy Spirit in every step as Teacher and with ourselves as learners and an active community of participants (chapters 4, 5).
2. DIVINE RESOURCES: It is grounded in increasing skill in the use of the Scriptures and prayer. The Scriptural resources are the foundational promises of God, continued listening to God through the Scriptures and the amazing resource of prayer (chapters 6 -8).
3. THE LEARNING JOURNEY: Learners own , share and surrender their journey together with others (learner agency, collaborative connection and risk agility). Formal teaching enables informal learning using methods adapted to learners' needs and preferences. Patterns are learned by imitation and not just theoretically taught. The formation of micro-teams manifests Jesus' presence as we learn and serve using experiential learning where Scriptural truth is transformed into life. Risk is learned progressively and in community (chapters 9 to 11).
4. SCALE: The discipleship fractal scales up to any size responding to the whole world, generation after generation while still accomplishing its' intended purpose. Disciples are made as the fractal progresses through each repetition. People are guided in what to do next with a story

they can remember allowing for communication across cultures and generations (chapters 3, 12, 13).

A suggested fractal

As you can see this is no small task to identify a fractal that can accomplish all or most of the above. Perhaps you would divide the resources a different way or change the labels of specific resources. Perhaps the cycle has fewer or more steps. Or maybe you would describe the kernel in different terms. Our task is to look into the Scriptures and figure out what pattern will bless our generation. What have we lost over time? What are we learning? How must the story evolve for the next generation? If we keep doing what we are doing, what is the emerging pattern?

For the sake of discussion let me present a diagram (figure 39) that attempts to capture these dynamics. You are invited to consider this fractal, improve upon it, and come up with something better.

You will notice there are 5 parts with what they represent:

- cross – the redemptive work of Christ, the kernel, and his example that we follow.
- world – the object of God's love and the goal of our commission.
- boxes – the learning journey that is integral to being a disciple. Notice the changing *I/we/they* dynamic and how *control* dynamically responds to the stages in the journey.
- pegs – the spiritual disciplines that transfers God's power from our lives to the world.
- arrows – the pathway that arrows that represent movement *upward* in worship, *outward* in loving service using our time, treasure and talents in micro-teams, and inward in spiritual growth both for ourselves and for helping others start the journey.

This fractal honours relationships by demonstrating the tension between personal responsibility (learner agency) and social interaction (collaborative connection). It also changes the learning paradigm from collecting information to practical obedience (risk agility).

It suggests a more realistic view of control issues, because learners must really own the responsibility for their life-long learning before they can honestly share and surrender it in the discipleship process. This removes discipleship from a programme mindset that must be controlled, to a relational and learner driven paradigm where disciples take charge of their learning and ministry to bless themselves, others and the world.

It suggests in scale-up where we do not simply "massify" the teaching but as we disciple individuals, we teach them to do the same in the journey inward. Appendix A has a study that can be used to discuss the inward journey with another. One can repeat the experience of helping others, imitating the dynamic of having received it.

This discipleship fractal is not something 'new' but is evidenced in the practices of the early church. At times the external organization has overshadowed the fractal or even replaced it with different repeating structures so that the patterns in the church may have conflicted with it.

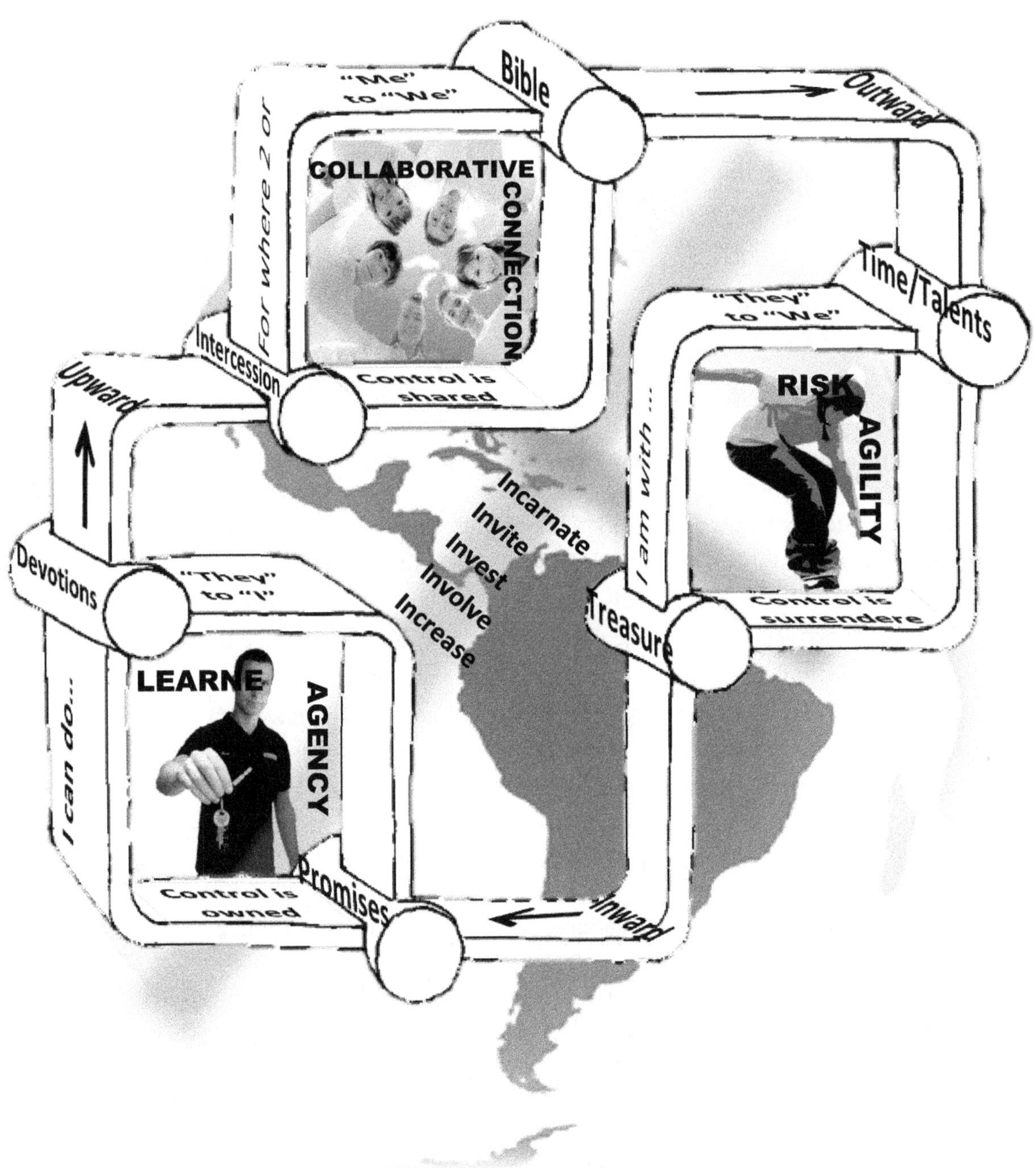

Figure 39: A suggested discipleship fractal

Obviously this fractal has problems. For one thing, spiritual growth is not as linear as the model suggests but much more a journey where we sojourn, live and grow. Also there is so much about God that is not symbolized by the cross: the love of the father, the grace and truth of the Son, the power of the Holy Spirit. Any reduction to one diagramme can be dangerous for all it leaves out.

I used to think that when it came to disciple-making, I wanted to be given the programme that worked and I wanted to measure numbers to evaluate success. These programmes often promised the sky but disappointed us or burnt out the leaders. Now I want to love people and learn together. I am much more concerned about the pattern of how we relate and much less concerned about final results which I feel is more of God's job. I want to find meaning in the process, learn on the journey and relate with others in Christ-like fashion.

Can we motivate and release the average follower of Jesus into a process like this? What would happen if leaders practice the discipleship cycle themselves, model what they are trying to reproduce and teach others to do the same? Imagine members accessing and integrating these divine resources and bringing their learning into their daily life and relationships? Imagine the release of creativity and initiative, the mobilization of millions of labourers and the redemptive influence in every corner of society. This is world changing.

The responsibility is for each of us to choose the fractal carefully that determines the patterns and results of our lives. The world clock is ticking away so it is not good enough to just be *busy* in the church but actively following Jesus' example. Fix your eyes on Jesus. He is our model, our method and our message. Cling to His promises. Find a few others with whom you partner no matter what. Break through a few roofs. Declare yourself free to learn even if you fail. Risk yourself to learn for Him, for yourself and for the world. Give this pattern to your children so they will see it lived and can choose wisely.

These discipleship fractals must also apply to the organization as well as individuals. We cannot sustain massive organizations that do not learn from the bottom up. These are not scalable. We must seriously evaluate unhelpful organizational fractals that resist the implementation of disciple-making patterns.

Thank you for joining me in this journey. I would love to hear from you what happens next in your adventure. Please consider participating online so we can learn together.[106]

For discussion:

1. What are the 'show-me-how' elements that you need to learn in order to make disciples? Or if you are a minister, what are the 'Show-me-how' things you are doing for the congregation?
2. Play with the Try Stuff fractal. How can it be scaled up?
3. Consider the healing of paralytic. How is this like an NCR fractal? What similarities do you observe and what is missing?
4. What fractal would you propose for disciple-making? What is your model? What tools do you propose using? How would you explain it to others?

[106] Instructions are given in the introduction of this book p.8.

5. Collect examples of how different people apply the discipleship fractal. I like the model by Jack Blanch:
   - Passionate prayer. Learn to stand before the throne of God with passion, faith and love.
   - Concerned listener. Learn to listen to the bad news before telling the good news. That means, hearing the other person's life story and their pain and need before offering a remedy.
   - Loving the lost. Change our attitude about the ungodly. Rather than disliking them, moving to compassion and love for them in their pain and confusion about life.
   - Praying community. Involve a community of believers in the process. Get a lot of people like yourself to pray. Don't go it alone.

For personal reflection:

Imagine viewing your grave stone. What legacy are you leaving? What risks would you wish you would have taken? What are you thankful for? What will you start doing differently from now on, knowing that you have been given the gift of living today? What fractal are you choosing?

Bibliography

Anderson, J., & McCormic, R. (2005, December 7). *Ten pedagogical principles for E-learning.* Retrieved March 21, 2011, from Insight: http://www.xplora.org/ww/en/pub/insight/thematic_dossiers/articles/quality_criteria/equality2.htm

Blackaby, H., Blackaby, R., & King, C. (2008). *Experiencing God: Knowing and Doing the Will f God.* Nashville: B7 H Publishing.

Blair, D. (2009, Vol 26 Issue 02). *Learner Agency: To understand and to be understood.* Retrieved from British Journal of Music Education: http://journals.cambridge.org/action/displayAbstract;jsessionid=C023069137E102E95A92B663025D9E76.tomcat1?fromPage=online&aid=5662584

Blanch, J. (2011, 2 23). Personal communication. Colorado Springs.

Burkhardt, H. (2010, June). *TOP 500 Supercomputing Sites.* Retrieved 1 19, 2011, from Top500.org: http://www.top500.org/lists/2010/06

Chip Heath, D. H. (2007). *Made to Stick: Why some ideas survice and others die.* New York: Random House.

Contestable, C. M. (2010, August). *Student and applied academics: Learner agency in a changing curriculum.* Retrieved 03 21, 2011, from InformaWorld: http://content.lib.utah.edu/cdm4/document.php?CISOROOT=/us-etd2&CISOPTR=158555

Covelli, M. (2010, 4 12). *The New Free Agent Learners.* Retrieved 3 21, 2011, from FTC 2010 Sessions: http://wire.wiscnet.net/2010/04/keynote-the-new-free-agent-learners-speak-up-about-emerging-technologies-and-21st-century-learning-with-julie-evans/

Duin, J. (2008). *Quitting Church: Why the faithful are fleeing and what to do about it.* Grand Rapids: Baker Books.

Elliot, M. (2009). *Confessions of an Insignificant Pastor*. Retrieved 1 18, 2011, from Doc Mark Elliot: http://www.docmarkelliott.com/

Eriksson, G. (2000, 4 20). *A study that is worth the effort*. Retrieved 2 1, 2011, from Amazon: http://www.amazon.com/Independent-Bible-Study-Irving-Jensen/product-reviews/0802439810/ref=dp_top_cm_cr_acr_txt?ie=UTF8&showViewpoints=1

Ginsberg, S. (2010, 10 20). *Hello My Name is Blog*. Retrieved 10 31, 2010, from http://www.hellomynameisblog.com/

Ginsberg, S. (2011, 1 19). *Hello My Name is Blog*. Retrieved from http://www.hellomynameisblog.com/

Gladwell, M. (2008). *Outliers: The Story of Success.* New York: Little, Brown and Company.

Jefferson, A. M., V.H.Pollock, R., & Wick, C. W. (2009). *Getting your Money's Wortth from Training and Development.* San Francisco: Pfiffer.

Klaas, J. H. (2007, 03 05). *Experiential Learning*. Retrieved 01 14, 2011, from YouTube: http://www.youtube.com/watch?v=mToQGltYXd8

Klaas, J. H. (2010, 11 11). *TRUST: Values for Self-organizing Learning*. Retrieved 2 7, 2011, from 1 Minute Learner: http://www.devedinternational.net/1ml/1ml-078/player.html

Maeda, J. (2006). *The Laws of Simplicity*. Cambridge, MA, USA: Massachusetts Institute of Technology.

Mandelbrot, B. W. (1982). *Fractals- A geometry of nature*. Retrieved 1 8, 2011, from Fortunecity: http://www.fortunecity.com/emachines/e11/86/mandel.html

McCormick, J. A. (2005, 12 7). *Ten pedagogical principles for e-learning*. Retrieved 3 21, 2011, from Insight: http://www.xplora.org/ww/en/pub/insight/thematic_dossiers/articles/quality_criteria/equality2.htm

McNabb, N. (2011, 3 25). personal communication.

Mohrbacher, N. (n.d.). *Will my baby get enough milk before my milk comes in?* Retrieved 2 1, 2011, from Ameda: http://www.ameda.com/breastfeeding/will-my-baby-get-enough-milk-my-milk-"comes-in"

Mowry, B. (2009). *The Ways of the Alongsider. growing Disciples Life2Life.*

Raymond, E. S. (2000). *The Cathedral and the Bazaar*. Retrieved 1 19, 20111, from http://www.catb.org/~esr/writings/cathedral-bazaar/cathedral-bazaar/

Sternin, J. (2007, 1 7). *The Positive Deviance Story*. Retrieved 3 25, 2011, from Policy Innovations for a fairer globalization: http://www.policyinnovations.org/ideas/innovations/data/PositiveDeviance

Trotta, D. (2011, 1 12). *Wikipedia, 10 years old, targets India*. Retrieved 1 14, 2011, from Reuters: http://www.reuters.com/article/idUSN1116765620110112?pageNumber=2

Virant, A. (2011, 1 28). My generation cares, and will deliver on the changes this world needs. *Guelph Mercury*, p. A12.

Wilcox, W. B., & Marquardt, E. (2010, December). *When Marriage Dissaperas*. Retrieved 1 12, 2011, from Universtiy of Virginia: http://stateofourunions.org/2010/SOOU2010.php

Witness. (2011, 1 13). *Wikipedia- 10 years on*. Retrieved 1 14, 2011, from BBC Podcasts: http://downloads.bbc.co.uk/podcasts/worldservice/witness/witness_20110113-0910a.mp3

Zimbardo, P. (n.d.). *Time, The Secret Powers of*. Retrieved 1 12, 2011, from YouTube: http://www.youtube.com/watch?v=A3oliH7BLmg&feature=channel

Appendix A

Spiritual Exercises in a Postmodern World

This four lesson exercise is designed to do together with another and then pass it on to help others in their spiritual journey and may be freely copied without changes for non-commercial use

The title page and each lesson should be folded separately. They can be used independently or assembled as a unit.

Download at: http://www.devedinternational.net/nwc/sepmw.pdf

www.ingramcontent.com/pod-product-compliance
Lightning Source LLC
Chambersburg PA
CBHW080216040426
42331CB00035B/3044

* 9 7 8 0 9 8 7 8 3 6 9 1 5 *